W9-BZV-982

DRINKING THE RAIN

Also by Alix Kates Shulman

NOVELS

In Every Woman's Life . . .

On the Stroll

Burning Questions

Memoirs of an Ex-Prom Queen

NON-FICTION

Red Emma Speaks: An Emma Goldman Reader

To the Barricades: The Anarchist Life of Emma Goldman

CHILDREN'S BOOKS

Finders Keepers

Awake or Asleep

Bosley on the Number Line

Drinking the Rain

ALIX KATES SHULMAN

FARRAR STRAUS GIROUX

NEW YORK

*Published simultaneously in Canada by HarperCollins*CanadaLtd
Printed in the United States of America
First edition, 1995

LIBRARY OF CONGRESS CATALOGING-IN-PUBLICATION DATA
Shulman, Alix Kates.
Drinking the rain / Alix Kates Shulman. — 1st ed.
p. cm.
1. Shulman, Alix Kates—Homes and haunts—Maine. 2. Women authors, American—20th century—Biography. 3. Women—Maine—Biography. 4. Islands—Maine. 5. Solitude. I. Title.
PS3569.H77Z47 1995 818'.5403—dc20 [B] 94-25693 CIP

This book is dedicated to
my brother Robert Davis Kates
(1931–1989), and to
Linda Trichter Metcalf,
sister and friend

CONTENTS

You do not need to leave your room. Remain sitting at your table and listen. Do not even listen, simply wait. Do not even wait, be quite still and solitary. The world will freely offer itself to you to be unmasked, it has no choice, it will roll in ecstasy at your feet.

—FRANZ KAFKA

PART ONE

The Island

ONE

THE tide is low, leaving a swath of damp, hard-packed sand as good as a dirt road for rolling my shopping cart along. Otherwise, the cartwheels would sink into the fine sand above the tide line or catch in the wrack, that dense tangle of seaweed, driftwood, shells, and debris that fringes the beach. The late-May sun is on its way down, spreading a vivid red glow across the sea and empty shore in starkest contrast to the life I've just left at the center of the continent's most worldly city. A city of eight million people speaking a combined total of eighty-nine human languages, of which I have command of one and a smattering of four. In this single day I've taken a journey encompassing subway, bus, jet, taxi, ferryboat, van, and finally shopping cart and my own two feet to wind up on a windswept beach at the tip of an island fifty minutes out to sea.

I've told everyone, myself included, I've come here alone for the summer to write. (By now my family understands how a writer needs solitude.) But secretly I already sense my excitement and fear are not about writing.

Halfway across the beach I stop at the point, face to the wind, to feel the ocean that circles the world crash at my feet. It seems prodigious, immense, far greater than the social forces that mold generations. As roar of subway yields to roar of surf, for a moment I want to hitch on to the ocean's force and coast.

But this is hardly a place for coasting. The cabin, perched by itself high on a green, rock-bound promontory known as the nubble, seems more like some piece of giant jetsam tossed up by an errant wave than the "charming vacation cottage" we touted in romantic ads when we occasionally rented it out. There's no plumbing, electricity, or heat in the cabin, no nearby neighbor, not even a road; the mail, picked up and delivered at a box on the other side of a tiny stream that separates this long beach from the nearest dirt road, takes a week to connect, and the island's only pay phone is half an hour's walk away, between the general store and the post office, near the ferry dock. That was fine for the brief family vacations we'd taken in years past, but my solo visit this summer is no vacation: I've come here not to vacate my life but to fill it.

NOT that my world seemed empty—if anything, it was more clogged than ever with busyness—but it had precipitously changed. This was in the early Eighties, years of glut and greed, when we who had come alive in one of the great liberation movements of the century, the liberation of women, watched helplessly as much that we had hoped to accomplish seemed to be arrested, forgotten, on the verge of being lost. The very word *feminist*, which we had rescued from the dungeon of ridicule where it had languished for decades, had been recaptured, bound, and gagged. Abortion rights had been steadily chipped away, violence spread, and the vision of equality that had inspired masses of us to organize in the Sixties and Seventies had been obscured by the alarming disparities between rich and poor, powerful and abused, that seemed only to increase with the passing years. All around me I could see a new generation taking over, and history, which my generation had passionately tried to shape, following its own unpredictable course. The faces were new, and in the bookstores I was shocked to find the newest books written by authors whose names I didn't recognize on subjects I'd failed to consider; reading them, I wasn't sure how to understand them.

I felt the decline of the women's movement as a personal loss, for my own work had grown in its nourishing soil; in my mind the two were hardly separable. The books I'd written and published in the dozen years since my first story appeared in a feminist journal owed their inspiration, subjects, and audience to the movement; it was my experience as an activist that had inspired the confidence I'd needed to write in the first place and gave me the sense that my work might, in however small a way, have some significance for others.

But as the world grew unfamiliar, I began to lose my bearings. I was unnerved when scholars started coming around with their tape recorders to take down my women's movement memories, then write monographs and dissertations about the campaigns, quarrels, and factional splits I'd witnessed, reducing my generation of activists to history—both literally and in the cruel slang of the young. Not that those young historians in their tailored suits weren't respectful, but, despite all the usual signs of time passing, I hadn't expected to become a relic so soon.

The facts were, my children were suddenly grown and gone; my husband, their father, who worked in a distant city, was increasingly estranged from me; my parents, though still vigorous in their age, were becoming fragile; friends had begun to die, and acquaintances I hadn't seen in a long time sometimes failed to recognize me. To spare them embarrassment, I rushed to say my name as soon as

I saw their puzzlement—or was it my own embarrassment I hoped to avert? I was entering my fifties, that ambiguous decade marking what's commonly considered in this country the beginning of the end for women. And though I had no less energy or vitality than before, every day it became clearer to me that the world which had grown young behind my back had a different view. More and more I found myself playing the number game: calculating how many years and decades had passed since certain events had occurred, noticing people's ages and achievements, comparing mine with theirs, theirs with mine, computing the proportion of my life I'd already lived and how much time might be left, feeling increasingly anachronistic, en route to obsolete, as, gradually, I became infected by the world's insidious opinion of aging women. I shuddered when I heard the names: old hen, biddy, little old lady in tennis shoes.

I was dismayed by these feelings, even ashamed, having always presumed that a good feminist would beat this rap. After so rewarding a life how unseemly was my anxiety—and I stubbornly fought it back. For years I'd been noticing how here and there some defiant one embraced fifty not as doom or disaster but as an opportunity, a staging area from which to begin an ascent. Approaching fifty Mother Jones, after losing her entire family to yellow fever, was reborn as a union organizer; at fifty the anarchist Emma Goldman was deported to the new Soviet Union where she hoped to help create the New Society; at fifty my friend Margaret F. left a bullying husband to become a midwife in a birthing commune in Mexico, and at fifty or so the famous Nearings moved from the city to Vermont to begin living the Good Life. Having like most women sensed the dire birthday coming from a long way off, I'd prudently prepared myself by vowing that I too would be reborn. Maybe this was just the compensatory fantasy of a politico whose movement had come and gone, or of a novelist with the habit of conceiving lives as narratives with turning points, climaxes, epiphanies, each marked by its own chapter. A self-fulfilling prophecy? No doubt my conviction that I would begin a new chapter might help it come true. But whatever my conscious intent, underneath I knew that no conviction or resolve can exempt anyone from what's coming. Even as I battled my fears with frenetic bursts of activity, whenever I slowed down I knew I was unprepared. I had assumed I'd always have work that mattered, would never be alone, but now my complacency gave way to astonishment that this obsolescence was happening to me, alternating with sorrow and, when I lost the confidence to write, dread. More than a year had passed since my last book was published and I was still floundering over the new one. Worst of all, as I felt myself growing superfluous, the world I'd once loved so fiercely started to lose its savor.

A flock of sandpipers running at the edge of the waves lures me from the point. I count fourteen of them. I follow them along the beach toward the nubble, a high, two-acre peninsula that protrudes like a thumb from the island at the juncture of two beaches. Every few feet the sandpipers skim forward just beyond my approach, leaving me behind as I hope I have left the world.

By the time I've lugged the cart through the dry sand across the nubble's neck up to the cabin steps I'm sweating. And apprehensive. Though there's nothing here worth stealing —the furnishings are mainly discards salvaged from the beach, the dump, or St. Joseph the Provider—I can't banish the image of the shambles that greeted us a dozen years before as we walked into the cabin: one of the main posts hacked and the hatchet gone, bloody Kotex smeared around the floor, the fire extinguisher spent, the screen doors slashed, dishes broken, bullet holes through an eye and ear of the deer head mounted over the door. No one ever "claimed credit" for the trashing. Someone suggested the assault had been directed against Mat Burns, who built our cabin in 1965 and had enemies on the island; but I always wondered if it wasn't against us, the island's only Jews.

One flight up from the beach I retrieve hammer, crowbar, and wrench from their hiding place under the cabin and begin to open up. First I open the valve on the propane tank and close the one on the rain barrel, then I climb another flight to the deck and pry off the winter boards covering the windows and doors and heave them down below, where tomorrow I'll stack them. Taking a breather, I lean on the railing to survey the double sweep of beach in the fading light and wonder why it has taken me so many years to get here by myself. And why I seldom came alone with just the children either, though they love this beach and we could have spent our summers here, since I'm a writer and, unlike my husband, not bound to an office.

Because I was afraid. Afraid not only of assault but afraid that hidden away I would be effaced, forgotten.

By whom?

By everyone I knew, but especially by my husband, who I was convinced would lose no time finding a replacement for me, temporary or otherwise. Afraid that if I slackened my pace for a moment I would be pushed off the road and left behind while the race went surging by. Having created around me in New York City a little world of which I was naturally the center, I dared not risk going to the periphery, where I might easily slip off the edge—as if the center of my life could somehow be outside myself; as if I needed to be witnessed to be real. So I had come here only for occasional family weekends with a houseful of city guests and, clinging stubbornly to the city, joined my voice to the rest who proclaim that a day away from New York is a day lost.

Staring at the empty beach I realize that, except for one month in Europe twenty-five years ago when I left my husband to travel by myself, I've rarely been alone for more than a few days in my entire life. Home, college, marriage, children . . . the woman's story of my class and generation. And pretty much of my mother's before me. And during that single month in Europe I panicked, asking myself incessantly: What are you doing here? What will become of you?

INSIDE, everything's just as we left it the summer before—floors swept, hearth clean, dishes stacked on the open shelves, a jar of dried flowers atop the great twelve-sided table that dominates the room, constructed by a proto-hippie carpenter friend from the wooden back of an abandoned truck and set upon four upturned elephantine logs. The pink Victorian piano, retrieved long ago from the island dump where a church had deposited it for recycling, is closed. Shells on the windowsills, Stevie's monster drawings on the wall. All silent, familiar, undisturbed.

I crank open the casements, replace the glass with screens in two of the eight storm doors, and go into action—check the radio and flashlight batteries, light the gas lamps and stove, reassemble the creaky pump that draws water into the sink from the rain barrel below the deck, and settle down on the floor with a box of kitchen matches to light the temperamental gas fridge. My husband, Jerry, who always took charge of the equipment, said I'd never manage this by myself. But half a box later the fridge is going, and I grab a bucket and dash down the two flights of outside stairs to collect kindling on the empty beach below while there's still light. Not the long South Beach I just came over but a secret beach hidden from the world unless you come by sea. Singing Sand Beach, it's called on the charts, and kicking off my sneakers I skid along barefoot to make it sing its eerie song, high and faint as the peep of a newly hatched chick, but steady, like a pennywhistle. A mixture of salt and iodine fills my nostrils as I suck in draughts of chilly air and fill my bucket with driftwood faggots. Most are too gorgeous to burn: a knot like an eye, burl like a wave, a forked branch like the bottom of a cowboy wearing chaps. Tentatively I divide them into burners and savers, remembering that until my first winter stay at an artists' colony eight years before I didn't know how to build a fire. And that leads me back to my seventh-grade science teacher, Mr. Armstrong, who officially dismissed the girls in his classes from the lessons on building motors since, he said, a boy could always build one for them.

Back in the cabin, watching the waves break on the rocks that a child long ago named Dedgers, I remember how, at other, earlier times, in the first hushed moments inside with everything simple and serene, I'd have an intimation of what might be possible here. But then the chores would begin, the whooping children would change into their swimsuits, guests would bounce on their cots, someone would mention food—and all fragile possibilities would fizzle in the fun. Fifteen years' worth of family visits to this nubble can do nothing to counter my sense that this is my first time—no more than years of reluctant sex can taint the newness of love.

As soon as I blow out the candle and snuggle down under two sleeping bags the night fears fly in—those fears I'd pooh-poohed when voiced by city guests but can't help heeding now that I'm alone: leaking gas that may explode, embers flying up the chimney to ignite the roof, accidents, illness, lightning, hurricanes, tidal waves, the deadly nightshade surrounding the cabin, beasts, rodents, and worst of all that roaming hacker who, one moonlit night, seeing a humble shack set high on a lonely point, will walk across the beach, climb the stairs, throw open the door, and hack us all to death. I've been expecting him for years. His gruesome crimes are reported daily on the news, and every woman who ever came here from the city to visit inquired if I was not afraid of him. In the city one escapes him in crowded streets and behind bolted doors, but in an isolated cabin with latches like toothpicks there's nothing to hold him back. For comfort I lift the baseball bat Jerry keeps as a weapon beside the bed, though I'll never dare use it. Some hackers, I try to console myself, seem to prefer a mob: dormsful of nurses, extended families of eight or ten, a busload. When I switch on the radio in search of soothing music, the main effect is simply to muffle the outside sounds, so I quickly snap it off and focus my attention on each rattle and creak until I'm unable to tell if the pounding in my ears is the surf, the hacker's footsteps, or my own thumping heart.

It's a long time before I fall asleep.

TAP, *tap, tap.* My lurching heart jolts me awake. Gaudy sun-drenched morning fills my eyes, adrenaline charges through my veins, diamonds on the water, loud tapping at the window. Someone trying to get in? I jackknife up in bed, peer out. Nothing. Another window, then? *Tap, tap, tap.*

Then it strikes me: this sharp repeated rap is no human sound but that of some creature who preceded me here, oblivious of my arrival. I've awakened in a country where I'm a mere visitor. All receptive and curious, eager to see the inhabitants and begin to sample the culture and cuisine, but humble, too, like any visitor who doesn't know the language.

I steal out of bed and creep stealthily to the main room for an unimpeded look at the row of windows. A small buff-and-yellow bird is ferociously attacking the glass, then retreating to the railing opposite until it has recovered sufficient strength to hurl itself once more against the glass, attacking with repeated exhausting thrusts of its sharp beak. I watch, riveted. It's dark above, white underneath, about four or five inches long, with bright yellow patches on its head and rump. One of those birds we indifferently called songbirds which always flitted through the dense brush of flowering shrubs and weeds between the bayberry bushes and the apple tree. But I have a field guide that could tell me exactly what it is and perhaps why it's so furiously attacking the window. I memorize its features and inch my way toward the bookshelf. Too quickly, too soon: the bird is gone before I can reach the book.

For a solid week I startle awake each dawn to the bird's mad assault upon the window, scattering my dreams. And though I soon identify it as a myrtle warbler, one of many living peacefully among the song sparrows and finches inhabiting the brush between here and the apple tree, I have no idea why it wants to break into the house. To reach a phantom nest? To peck out the eyes of its own reflection? To harass me off its property? But going to sleep at night wondering if the bird will be attacking the window in the morning does take the edge off hypothetical attacks, and by the day the bird stops coming, releasing me to walk straight past the window to the sink to prime the pump and fill the kettle, the hacker has moved from the center of my fantasies to a dark place beneath the cabin. Now only occasionally —especially when the wind is up—I think I hear him move about or knock a board as he bides his time.

I intended to get down to work immediately, knowing how dangerous are unscheduled days, how fragile self-imposed plans. Facing the vast expanse of an entire summer alone, aware of the same nervous tick of time that had always dogged me in the city—that nagging countdown, time, money, achievement—I was ready to invoke the god of discipline. I knew well enough how I ought to proceed: arrange my papers, review what I'd written so far, and begin—as I'd done each time I'd gone to an artists' colony, where my efficiency had always doubled or tripled simply because I was out of New York.

New York: where the calendar is full for weeks on end and no sooner does one month pass than another is beckoning with its stimulating meetings, panels, symposia; where every day the post brings fresh announcements from the Events Committee, invitations from sponsors of urgent causes, stirring appeals, public statements to be signed and supported; where visiting writers and new exiles arrive each week needing to be heard; where documentaries and retrospectives beckon to their limited runs. Not to mention the manuscripts, galleys, advance copies of new books begging to be blurbed or reviewed, the urgent conversations with friends.

My activist soul once welcomed the stuffed mailbox and ringing phone as opportunities, despite my writerly need for solitude. But as the women's movement fizzled, revealing that the world we had hoped to change *now* would always need changing, they began to feel more like distractions and intrusions enforced by threats of guilt. The price of a full life seemed to be a cluttered life until finally, as I began to understand that such duties and pleasures could never be fulfilled in my lifetime, I stuffed a suitcase, put a hold on my mail, and walked away, as if for a coveted month of work at the MacDowell Colony, where the single inviolable rule is that no one may ever visit your studio without an invitation. Only, here, at my colony, there's no breakfast waiting when I wake up, no staff to prepare and serve candlelit dinners or silently deliver lunch in a picnic basket to my doorstep or pile firewood and kindling unbidden on my porch, and after a hard day's work no evening concert in a library or literary conversation over dinner, no community, friendship, or lover. Here for company there'll be nothing but books, a small portable radio, and myself.

This nubble retreat is more pared down than any I have gone to before, even more than the Millay Colony where four years ago my family dropped me off for one month with nothing but a small bag of clothes and a portable typewriter. How terrified I was when we drove up the mountain in the Berkshires to find only a big empty barn and snow-covered fields and no one to greet me. How different from the civilized MacDowell. I searched through the barn. Four sparsely furnished rooms, all empty, all freezing, two with beds, two with desks, and an unfinished bathroom with a plastic shower stall. There were supposed to be three artists at this colony, but only two beds? The only sign of life was some mouse turds in a bureau drawer. Maybe I had the wrong month, the wrong mountain. "Wait!" I cried, running outside as I heard Jerry start up the car. "Don't leave me here alone!" I tried to smile but I was only half joking —like the time when, at nine, I hitchhiked back home after the first night of summer camp, pretending I was above it all, but actually unbearably homesick. I held on to the car door and would probably have thrown my bags and typewriter back in the trunk, climbed into the front seat, and gone straight home if Stevie and Amy hadn't been there to witness my example. After all, my children were about to spend the entire month of May without a mother, possibly a more traumatic dislocation than my own, and I had already kissed them goodbye. So I let them go, and I calmed down, and eventually two more artists did show up, a poet with whom I shared the barn and a painter who slept and worked behind the kitchen in another building where we all ate together and consoled each other in our loneliness, and by the end of the month spring had flowered on that mountain and we had become friends. But there were three of us—plus the director of the place and the vivacious, sociable Norma Millay, aged sister of the poet, who sometimes invited us to lunch and if coaxed gave dramatic readings of her sister's poems in her gravelly sonorous voice, explaining a line here, telling a story there, relentlessly lighting another cigarette with her wrinkled hands, tossing back her long still-golden hair as if she were once again, as in the Twenties, back on stage at the Provincetown Playhouse on MacDougal Street, one of the celebrated Millay sisters, toast of Greenwich Village, burning the candle at both ends. There were three of us then, but here my colony has only one visitor, myself, who also doubles for staff.

Then to work! I arrange my papers in an orderly fashion on my driftwood desk and sharpen my pencils, as I always do. But instead of sitting down to work, I do something I've never done before. I take the saw from its hook, search through the woodbox for a few slim boards, and saw several makeshift bookshelves for the books and papers I've mailed up ahead of me. It's tough going; I have no experience or technique. But I want those shelves, so I persist. When I'm done the shelves are a bit uneven, but they please me all the same. I wedge them between the wall studs and nail them in.

I still don't sit down to work. Instead I gather up all the books in the cabin to order and rearrange. Which means making still more shelves—searching the woodbox, woodshed, and beach for the right boards, sawing them to size, nailing them in place, admiring them. And once I've organized the books, I rearrange the other shelves with their shells, rocks, food.

Now when the sun streams into my bed at dawn my energy propels me not to my desk, as it did in the city, but to the kitchen, the deck, the storeroom, the beach, the woods—anywhere, it seems, *but* my desk.

This is something new. Haven't I come here to work? I'm a writer; writing is what I do. For a dozen years, despite teaching, political work, and mothering, scarcely a day has passed that I have not set pen to paper to express my mind or heart. My files are stuffed with my imaginings, published and unpublished. Notebooks filled margin to margin with my tiny scrawl spill out of the desk drawers. Cartons of my papers and notes rest in an Ohio attic. The thousands of books in my library bear on their flyleaves and in their margins traces of my thoughts. When I'm not writing—that is, when no pen is in hand or keyboard under my fingertips—I'm likely to be musing, mulling, meditating, composing—with writing instruments never out of reach. I chew up pencils. I spit out my dreams, faithfully recording them in the dream book I keep beside my bed, so that even in the middle of the night every waking moment can be spent at productive work. Pens and pencils are everywhere, beside the bed, on each table, in a jar in the kitchen among the spices, piled on the desk and in all the drawers. In every coat and jacket pocket, stuffing all my purses and in the pockets of my traveling bags are writing instruments, notebooks, scribbled scraps of paper.

Perhaps I need some time to settle in before I can begin to write. And for the first time ever, I allow myself the reckless thought that it may not matter if I write or not: with no one here to judge me, discovering what exactly I will do may be a more interesting project than writing a book.

I sit on the deck, bundled up against the breeze, shelling the tiny young beach peas I've just gathered to augment my lunch. A gray gull carries some sea creature high up over the beach, drops it from its beak. I stop to watch. Even before the splat, the gull shapes its wings into a parachute and drops straight down to eat the scattered remains.

And what will send me soaring and plunging? I want to avoid contaminating the answer by imposing my will but simply watch patiently and see. I'm prepared to slow down, wait, even stop—whatever it takes to get a true reading. Into my mind pops an image from an old Betty Grable movie in which a silly chorus girl who keeps her body in constant motion is transformed from a nervous striver into a dreamy torch singer when the hero, just before the curtain goes up, handcuffs her to the stage set and forces her to stand still. I have five or six months before the winter chases me away. Five or six months to slow down and learn to sing.

Slowing down and standing still—dreaded symptoms of age. But *old* is a moving target, receding like the horizon as you approach it. "A socially constructed disease with an adolescent onset," in the witty formulation of M. M. Gullette. I'd felt it coming on at twenty-five—"a quarter of a century old," I'd lamented then. Yet now, looking back on this adventure from the vantage point of sixty, fifty seems young—too young for the heavy weight I piled on it, only slightly less young than my mother considered it from the vantage of nearly eighty. The "perfect" age, she'd pronounced it—"young enough to have your full powers, but old enough to know."

To know what? Maybe if I slow down enough I'll find out.

Another gull swoops down and begins to hector the first one for its food. After a little noisy back and forth, the first one picks up its catch and flies off to a nearby rock to eat it undisturbed.

THAT night, for the first time since my arrival I dream a long-familiar recurring dream. In it I open a hidden door at the back of a closet or next to the refrigerator or behind the bed in my crowded life and climb a secret stairway to a whole new wing or floor known only to me. It is furnished with everything I might ever need and there are always rooms to spare. Rooms for each of the children, a study for me, a game room, a music room, a rec room, guest rooms, pantries, kitchen, library, hallways, hidden rooms, and rooms off rooms. All empty, except for me. How, I wonder, could I not have known (or remembered) it was here. I wander from room to room, filled with secret delight.

This dream is so familiar that sometimes, even in my sleep, I recognize as I discover the door that I'm about to enter it, and everything seems possible. The rooms are always surprising, different from one dream to the next. Sometimes they peel off a long, dark corridor to the right and left. Sometimes they surround a high-ceilinged ballroom with crystal chandeliers. Occasionally they give onto a wide balcony that overlooks the sea. No matter—the pleasure I feel as I settle in for the dream is invariably the same: astonishment, sweet joy, contentment.

What do I do there in my rooms before I descend the stairs, return through the door, and wake? What do I do? At first I just walk from room to room, amazed. At the luxury of so much empty space, at my unbelievable luck. Then, after the initial surprise, for as long as I can make the dream last I am simply there.

A violent thunderstorm wakes me. It goes on for an hour, sending rapid strobes of light across the bed where I lie under my sleeping bags; it shakes the rafters with thunderclaps, cracking across the sky like an overseer wielding a brutal whip, whipping up the sea.

At first I concentrate my fears on fire, reliving all the nights I've lain there figuring out escape routes, picturing each of the children as a casualty, trying to remember how to activate the fire extinguisher. No doubt this wooden structure, built out of driftwood beams, rough-sawn timber, used windows and doors, cheap Masonite floors, sitting high on a bluff, is a lightning rod and firetrap—and no water supply, no phone to summon help, not even a road for a fire truck to race across. But with no children to protect, I soon drop my guard and walk to the window where I stand watching silver waves crash against the rocks of Dedgers as lightning rips open the sky.

The storm shakes me, like the scare that shook me up a year ago, tearing me from the commonplace. An acute attack of dizziness while doing my sit-ups. I remember staggering to bed, but the room continued to spin, leaving me nauseated and frightened. Next day the doctor prescribed small yellow pills for vertigo. Two weeks later the dizziness was still there, and after a month the world still looked like an underwater cave through which I was rapidly floating on a spiraling moving stair. After doing all I could to deny whatever it was, after abandoning the yellow pills as ineffective, after reconstructing the fall that had raised a red plum on my bleeding head, there seemed to be no more possibility of waking from this fantasy turned nightmare. I can still see the doctor slowly shaking his trim little beard as he invited me from the examining room into his office and wrote on a prescription pad like a death sentence the name of the specialist to whom he was handing me over for "a complete neurological workup." All at once my numberless days were numbered. I looked at the address: a hospital way uptown, near the Bronx.

As soon as I was out of the doctor's office and back on the windy street I had two simultaneous, competing thoughts, one glum, one giddy: first, I have been sentenced to spend my few remaining days riding the subway back and forth between the two ends of Manhattan; second, I needn't finish writing my recalcitrant book but am free to do anything I choose.

I shoved the address in my coat pocket and turned homeward. I had to phone my husband, warn my parents. The children? At the thought of them, tears started to my eyes and joined the wind to blind me. I brushed them away, held out my hands: cold but steady. Heartbeat: normal. I seemed to be feeling . . . nothing, or nothing I might be expected to feel. Was this self-observation a reflex of terror—some deep denial of the inevitable?

Denial never works. Hadn't I always secretly known this moment would come? Yes, I always knew, trembled each time I read *Everyman*, studied Tolstoy and Eliot, Goethe and Woolf, gave up cigarettes, caffeine, cholesterol, panicked on highways and shuddered in small planes. I dreaded the ocean, feared dogs, dishonor, and drunks. Always ready to knock on wood, throw salt over my shoulder, bite my tongue, cross my fingers. Why then had I done nothing to prepare (fear is not preparation but the opposite), living my lives profligately as if there would always be another about to be born, as if life were an unlimited resource to be spent and spent? Suddenly the time was up. The lives I'd lived had piled up behind me into a messy heap and blown away like a giant tumbleweed: children grown, friends, mostly young, oblivious of death, and my aged parents—how could I burden them with the untimely funeral of their youngest child?

Alone with this possible death of mine, alone with a straight shot at the end, I had to decide what to do. Should I rush out to fulfill my obligations? cling to what I had? project myself onto the living through last wishes and legal instruments? settle my debts? dash to finish my manuscript or in a fling of liberation burn what I had? Or should I throw off all restraints and strike out on my own?

Like everyone, I'd often played at guessing what I'd do if suddenly told:

—you have just won a million dollars

—you are banished to a desert island and may take with you a single book

—you have ten months left to live

but it no longer felt like a game. I reread the address where the brain scans were to be run and decided that if I had only a limited time left on earth I would not spend it in a subway riding back and forth to a hospital.

For the first time the image of the hospital itself entered my thoughts. The hospital, that sterile stinking fluorescent hell where you've dreaded even to visit, much less reside, knowing you'd be captive not only of bureaucrats and doctors but of every unwanted relative you avoided in your arrogant immortal days but now must helplessly watch push through the door smiling, gloating, glowing with health. They lean close, breathing in your face, bringing hateful sweets and flowers and every boring story and futile bit of advice you have anticipated or already heard when you need to be alone to think. And leading the pack of them, your husband, with whom you had worked out a livable arrangement, spending most of your time apart, but whose directorial presence, now that you are captive, is intolerable. Admit it at last, even though he is father to your children. Admit it, at the price of being rudely remembered: entertaining with a smile is not the way to exit from this world, even if the uninvited guests are your own family with their ancient claims on you.

Away, away, away! Is the mileage in my frequent-flyer account enough to carry me away before it's too late? (If not, may I will my miles, or must I take them unused to the grave?) I remember the places where it was said one could go to have the baby during pregnancy scares of half a world ago—the only solution short of suicide. How soothing was the thought of anonymity in a strange city where you could stay long enough after the birth to get back your shape—the same city where, reputedly, you could leave behind snippings of your old nose and emerge a new person. But not, apparently, pieces of a damaged brain.

I think of my friend Toby, who confided to me on the morning before his triple-bypass surgery: "I've learned two major things from my heart attack. The first one is, if I survive this surgery I'll never rush again. The second is this, I'm going to show my love as often as I can."

Like Toby, I recovered from my death scare, but not until it had sounded a warning that I heeded with a different vow. Though not so dire as some people's warnings—no open-heart surgery or HIV—the virus I survived was nonetheless frightening enough to remember even after I woke up one day to find that the shaky vertiginous sea I'd been wobbling through had gone out like a tide as unexpectedly as it had come, leaving me solidly back on terra firma. With my new footing I climbed to the highest point in sight and from there surveyed the past and future as far as I could see. My sickness had improved my vision by several degrees, making me less nearsighted in one eye, less farsighted in the other. And what I saw was this: you only have one life, which, though brief, is long enough if you use it well. I vowed to find out how.

The storm ends as abruptly as it began. An arc of light marks the rim of white beach where the waves peter out; the roar subsides, the night turns calm. Although the moon is concealed behind a cloud, three lighthouses spaced like sentries on the black horizon join the lowing foghorns to protect the island and its invisible sleeping inhabitants. I feel their presence from my high lookout. Even this isolated nubble, all but enclosed by a circle of silver waves like a child in utero, seems protected from every possible assault; and when the moon comes rolling back into full view like a benediction, I feel somehow purged and safe.

Back in the bedroom I pick up the bat from beside my bed, carry it out on the back deck, and with both hands heave it onto the woodpile. There it lies in the moonlight, benign as any other log on the heap. After grappling with death, what worse is there to fear? If one day I should hear the hacker's slow, booted step on the stair, perhaps I'll suggest a cup of tea and try to get the story of his life.

TWO

IT was almost by accident that I discovered the hidden treasures of the nubble. Chance, coupled with rebellion and a touch of laziness. Do only what you like, nothing you don't! became my new motto, and I disliked the hour-long trek to and from the store. It was a drag to drag that dying shopping cart up and down the hills several times a week to transport, at best, only wilted produce and a few basics. I hadn't come to the end of the world to go shopping.

I'd never liked to shop. From the time I fled Ohio in the early Fifties for my beatnik apprenticeship in New York City, embracing mind and eschewing "things" had been my self-defining strategy, one that, through the mysterious imperatives of culture, deemed sensual pleasures (good) and material possessions (bad) mutually exclusive. Even after I relinquished bohemia for family life, when Stevie and Amy were little I ordered the family clothes from the Sears catalogue, though we were right there in the middle of Manhattan surrounded by boutiques. Food shopping I liked better, with all the ethnic specialty shops and neighborhood markets in New York City, and when a farmers' market opened nearby on Union Square I looked forward to the pleasures of squeezing vegetables and sampling fruits on

Saturday mornings. But there were none to squeeze at the island store.

That was a pity for someone as passionate about food as I. In fact, it was through food that I'd first learned to gobble up the world after a childhood as an indifferent eater. To this day my memories of a transforming student year in Europe, when my husband was a Fulbright and I a "half-bright," as wives were called, are as dense with the taste of food—my first artichoke, my first celery-root salad with my first rémoulade sauce, my first weisswurst and prosciutto—as with images of pissoirs along the grand Parisian boulevards, the bombed-out streets of Munich, flamenco dancers on the outskirts of Spanish villages, the young wolves representing Remus and Romulus pacing their Roman cage on Michelangelo's Campodoglio. Other people show snapshots and slides when they come home, but I, returning to New York in 1957, with missionary zeal taught myself to cook in order to make monthly European feasts for friends not lucky enough to have gone abroad in those days when transatlantic travel was prohibitively expensive, when a broiled steak dinner represented the pinnacle of celebration, when Italian food meant spaghetti swimming in tomato sauce. The first person in my family to cross the ocean going east, I felt a calling to introduce my compatriots to such wonders of nature as blood oranges, snails, squash flowers, and fennel. To me food was part of the great postwar cultural adventure: mind-expanding and sensual, titillating and educational, like atonal music, or experimental sex, or marijuana, or a new language, only more readily accessible, and I wanted to share the thrill of the flavors of French, German, and Italian food that had taken me completely by surprise. As Marco Polo had brought back noodles from China to Italy, so I brought spaghetti alla carbonara from Rome to provincial young New Yorkers.

Returning home every evening from my editorial job to cook dinner for my graduate-student husband was a comedown after the adventure of cooking in Europe. I missed the excitement of setting off of a morning to fill my string bag with each new offering of the butcher, the baker, the greengrocer, the sausage-maker of München–Obermenzing, often returning home with the grocer's personal recipe. Then one happy day I discovered the long stretch of Greek, Italian, and Middle Eastern markets in Hell's Kitchen on Ninth Avenue, collectively called Paddy's Market, where I immediately took to spending my precious Saturdays grocery shopping. Strolling before the pushcarts and laden windows felt something like being in another country: Syrian bakeries displayed baklava in pans made of the empty film cans discarded by the documentary-film industry that shared the neighborhood; greengrocers sold kale, chard, mustard, turnip, dandelion, and other unnamed greens, unobtainable in those days at the A&P but redolent of the mysterious wild "field salads" I had so recently enjoyed in Europe. One butcher shop sold veal chops with the kidney attached, another displayed lamb's heads, sweetbreads, trotters, and small round organs which my youthful eye had already identified as some poor creature's testicles. Pointing, I asked the butcher in my most innocent voice, "What're those?" The butcher smiled, summoned two of his colleagues with a wave of his hand, and answered as innocently, "Mountain oysters." "Oysters?" I asked incredulously. "Really? How do I cook them?" Grinning now for his buddies: "You just slice them up, dip them in a little egg, coat them in bread crumbs or flour"—clapping imaginary slices between almost floury palms—"fry them up in a little butter. Salt and pepper, maybe some chopped garlic—but better not tell your boyfriend." "I'll take a dozen," I said, barely able to hide my glee, already planning new hors d'oeuvres for that weekend's lucky guests.

The next year, while we were driving through Castroville, California, a town that proclaimed itself on banners stretched across Main Street to be the "Artichoke Capital of the World," my culinary proselytizing took a new turn. My own introduction to artichokes had occurred on my first night in Paris in the plain little bistro where my husband and I and another couple from our student ship stopped for our first French dinner. Perplexed, we surreptitiously watched the people at the next table pull apart with their fingers, petal by petal, a dense upright green flower, then dip each petal in melted butter and draw it sharply between their teeth. When the petals' ragged remains were piled in unsightly heaps at the sides of their plates, they carefully scraped the flower's center and ate with knife and fork what we soon learned to call the heart. I was surprised to find an American town dedicated to this European delicacy. Quite sure my parents and their siblings, in Cleveland all their lives, had never seen, much less eaten, an artichoke, I shipped my deprived family a twenty-five-pound bargain case. To spare them the unpleasant sensation of a mouthful of choke that attended my own imperfect initiation, I sent them a letter introducing my strange gift and instructing them, with the help of line drawings, how to prepare, cook, and eat the unfamiliar treat.

Years later, cooking daily for two sometimes finicky children, I lavished on their lunches all the creativity I could summon by making food pictures on their plates, sketching a basic landscape of egg yolk for sun, egg whites for snow, carrots for tree trunks, spinach for grass, lettuce for leaves, cheese for clouds. And though years of cooking several meals a day dampened my initial enthusiasm, still I tried to master an ever wider range of tasty basics and nutritious frills for a family of constantly shifting tastes who needed to be fed every single day. That experience helped me understand why so many people consider cooking a chore and daily domestic life limiting, why they prefer frozen dinners, restaurants, fast foods, takeout. I understood the taint that adheres to everything domestic. It's not simply a matter of drudgery or tedium—not with some of the loudest complaints coming from those with domestic help, or the single and childless who may eat as they choose and whose chores are limited. It's the taint of the female. How do I know? When a man cooks, when a man is domestic, in place of the taint there's honor.

But I never stopped cooking gladly, not even after the children grew up and left home. Unlike most of my single friends, who claim to enjoy cooking only for guests, taking what solitary meals they can afford in the sociable atmosphere of cafés and restaurants, I find every meal I prepare for myself an opportunity. After decades of providing food for the lowest common denominator among the family's disparate tastes, of sometimes suffering stage fright when called upon to cook for company, of occasionally feeling sad that my services are taken for granted, I rejoice to indulge no other taste but mine. Alone, I can make a feast of a single dish or an adventure of an experiment gone awry. Give me a kitchen and an appetite and I may do anything—snack or fast, consume seven-course banquets or lunch on peanut-butter sandwiches.

But if I can manage with fewer trips to the store, so much the better.

Part of my plan to avoid shopping entails eating the local mussels—if I can find them again. Back when we first began coming to the island, mussels were so plentiful that I pressed on favored guests bagfuls of the medium-sized blues I blithely picked from one of three large tidal pools crammed with the succulent bivalves visible at a glance through the clear water. With tiny seed mussels in every little crevice, none of us dreamed they would disappear but assumed that as fast as we could pick the large ones the small ones would grow up to take their place.

Then one summer we returned to Maine to find the colony greatly thinned and the next summer, gone. Behind our urban backs, without notice or forwarding address, our mussels had mysteriously disappeared.

Had we picked too profligately? Had the bivalves, seemingly so hardy, been overcome by some hostile organism or oil spilled by one of the big tankers now frequenting Portland harbor? Or had they simply picked up and moved to some other cove? Rachel Carson's explanation is that in very cold winters the rocks may be scraped clean of barnacles, mussels, and seaweeds simply by the mechanical action of ice grinding in the surf, after which it may take several growing seasons separated by moderate winters before the creatures return. But back then no book or neighbor enlightened me. Crestfallen, I desultorily hunted near my now empty pools for mussels large enough to pick, but none turned up, and soon I stopped looking. No one else seemed to care. With store food to eat and plenty of empty shells to collect during our brief annual visits, they considered mussels only an extra, anyway. In subsequent years my hopes were occasionally rekindled by the reappearance of tiny seed mussels, so small that ten of them could cover my smallest fingernail. But they didn't seem to grow from one year to the next, and, doubting that they would ever achieve an edible size, I gave up my search.

That was all years ago; now I'm ready to try again. I'm

sure there are mussels here because I see their empty shells. And not only mussels. Big clams, steamers, razor clams, even an occasional lobster claw or a scallop, and once a prized oyster shell. Plus sea urchins and crabs dropping from the beaks of high-flying gulls who swoop down to feast on them. But how shall I, a mere human, find such creatures inside their shells, alive?

When the tide is low and the sun high, I set off with a bucket to circle the nubble. Everything leaps with new life: sandhoppers scoot across the beach like tiddledywinks, gulls bark and strut out on the rocks. In the bay, where lobster buoys bob in the waves, a pair of ducks put six ducklings through their diving paces. Upending rocks in the muddy cove, I uncover fighting green crabs that rise up startled and scurry off into the muck. Following a hermit crab traveling under a dog-whelk shell, I come upon hundreds of periwinkles feeding on a giant strand of kelp. I poke a twig into a hole that squirts a stream at me—and soon I've forgotten about mussels.

After lunch I set off to search in a different direction. But again I'm quickly distracted, this time by the new spring growth of ferns beginning to unfurl, young dandelions sprouting among the flat rocks of Skip Stone Beach, three perfect blue wild irises. By the time I've made my way to the rocks the tide is halfway in, and again I return home musselless.

Now I'm getting hungry. The following morning I'm careful to go down to the shore when the tide is going out so I can explore the entire circumference of the nubble before it flows back in. This time I ignore the ducks and cormorants fishing in the bay, hurry past the unfolding flora, and wander far out onto the rocky backside of the nubble. I don't remember this lunar landscape, with pocks like giant footprints in the jagged rocks, accessible only during dead low tide. It's treacherous going, with layers of wet rockweed disguising hidden fissures. I slide on the slippery seaweed, stumble, fall; still I press on toward the farthest rocks at the water's edge.

And suddenly, stepping down between two large shoreline boulders, I find myself staring into a clear pool filled with hundreds of the largest blue mussels I've ever seen, restaurant color and market size. I'm Robinson Crusoe on his island sighting sheep, feeling saved.

This particular pool is far from the pools where we used to hunt, and as I settle back on my heels to pick the barnacly blues, I wonder why in my search I never came this way before. As one at a time I twist and tug the mussels loose, strip off their fuzzy beards, rub their shells against a stone to rid them of barnacles, and plop them into my bucket, I wonder if perhaps they've been here all along, like the fabled secret garden, and not they but I—inattentive, impatient, busy—constitute the variable.

I sit on the deck eating mussels straight from the pot, spooning up the rich salty broth in a shell, watching the sun go down. They're the firmest, most succulent mussels I've ever had. I've cooked them as we used to years ago, steamed in an inch of water with chopped garlic and onion; only, these taste better. Each one is an adventure, so stimulating to palate and mind that having rediscovered them I fancy their becoming my new staple, replacing meat, with its globules of grease filming every dish, so messy to clean in a house without hot running water and so chancy to preserve in my unreliable fridge.

I think back to the mountains of meat we used to consume

in one long weekend with guests. Sausages, bacon, chickens, hot dogs, hamburgers, steaks, ribs, chops. Plus canfuls of tuna, pâtés, soups, beans, coffee; boxes of Jell-O, marshmallows, chocolate, pasta, cereal, crackers, cookies, cakes, tea bags; cartons of milk, juice, ice cream; jars of ketchup, mustard, pickles, peppers, olives, jams, peanut butter, toppings; packages of paper towels and napkins, plastic plates and cups; bottles of water and booze; cases of soda and beer; bagfuls of fruits, greens, sweet corn, tomatoes, cucumbers, carrots, onions, potatoes, cheese, chips, buns, breads and more, along with Off for the mosquitoes, Raid for the ants, rat poison for the field mice who wintered over in the house, Cutters for us. Some guests even brought the Sunday *New York Times* and, after smearing themselves with sunblock, spread blankets on the sand and (unlike the locals who prefer to stand facing down the sea) lay in the sun in their stylish swimwear as if this beach were on fashionable Long Island, New York, instead of rugged Long Island, Maine.

I would try to put everything away immediately so as to be ready for the first production-number breakfast Jerry directed. He'd fire up the woodstove, then get down the giant four-burner skillet and lay in bacon or sausage, leaving me to drain the fat and fry up batch after batch of pancakes, or dozens of eggs to serve with buttered toast (tricky to avoid burning under the broiler), pitchers of milk, syrup, reconstituted frozen orange juice, drip coffee. No sooner was one meal consumed than it was time to begin preparing another. Every last bite hauled across the beach, the mounds of garbage and trash hauled back out again.

To gather everyone at mealtime Jerry ceremoniously rang a great brass ship's bell. Like the deer head mounted over the door, it had come from his parents' house in New Jersey, where both trophies had been left by the explorer who'd owned the house before them. He also used the bell to summon shirkers from their resting places, assigning each one a chore in his current home-improvement project. Even the rare moments of repose were filled with plans. I picture Jerry still, sitting on the deck with his hands clasped behind his head and his feet up on the railing, his chair tilted back against the wall, evaluating the view; or else leaning forward, large and unmoving, his feet planted firmly on the deck and his hands braced against his meaty thighs, like a ship's captain at the wheel, steering the house and all its personnel.

I resented all of it. Resented Jerry's buying the nubble in the first place, over my vehement opposition. Dreaded the tense six-hour drive to and from New York with a carful of bickering kids (ours and their friends), Jerry driving way too fast, the inevitable frantic rush for the ferry. I resented lamps too high for me to light, no way to do laundry, shoes lost to the tides, the constant fear of running out of water and supplies, having to watch the children every moment —all in pursuit of some mad idea of fun. Though I usually managed to suspend my resentment and enjoy myself (for the children's sake if not my own), sometimes I admitted I actually hated it here.

Now, with blue mussels available for the picking and as many ways to prepare them as my imagination can concoct, who needs meat? Years before, as part of a group of political activists and writers invited to visit China, I sat down to a spectacular duck banquet in Beijing, hosted by Chinese dignitaries. Between potent mao-tai toasts, we were served seventeen separate courses, each one featuring another part of the duck, including everything from grilled heads and beaks to the webs of the feet. Why should mussels, so delectable in soups, stews, paellas, and pastas, prove any less versatile? If I never pick more than I can eat in a day, then, with a guest list limited to one, perhaps I can live out the summer on the protein of this unexpected bounty.

THE next morning at six I'm as eager to get down to the shore as I've ever been in the city to get to my desk. I have a rough mental map of the location of my mussel pool. But the looks of the coast are deceiving: the configurations of land and ocean present entirely different worlds at different times of day, depending on the tides, the mists, the seasons, the sun and moon. The island's ten-foot-high tides, acting like a magic carpet, transform the shore twice each lunar day from a narrow strip of exposed beach between cabin and sea to a vast span of fine white sand stretching far away to seaweed-fringed coves and dark mudflats and hidden pools teeming with life. Jagged outcroppings cloaked in barnacles and rockweed change constantly from barely perceptible ripples on the waves passing over them to self-contained islands (named the Tinies by the children but by me the Shmoos) to miniature mountains hugging the shore. And try as I might to retrace yesterday's route, I can't find my mussel pool today.

Where is it? The tide leads me a strenuous chase, ducking behind boulders, tripping through shale moonscapes and across slippery seaweed traps, throwing me off the trail until it sidesteps neatly into the sea, leaving no trace of my pool. Baffled and frustrated, I refuse to give up but wade through the muck searching until at last I begin to see them—not in the large pool I expected but in surprising new places: a trio of mussels here, a small clump there hidden under rockweed, in crevices among the rocks, clinging to the base of a boulder. I bend and squat, feeling among the rocks and weeds, and just before the tide washes in, I have my dozen.

Amy, my daughter, has a knack for finding four-leaf clovers. "You can't find them by searching," she says to anyone who asks. "You have to just . . . sort of . . . glance down like this and one will be there"—and invariably she stoops and plucks a perfect four-leaf clover from the carpet of grass. This power that enables her to spot the prize every time, even from afar, this glance that approaches its object not directly but askance, is now amazingly mine for mussels. Like her, knowing they're there I can always find them. I think of the Sufi tale of the master archer renowned for always hitting a bull's-eye. What's your secret? begs the novice. It's easy, replies the master. I shoot my arrow, and wherever it lands I draw a bull's-eye around it.

Now each day I wake up tuned to mussels. As soon as the tide is right, I tie on a wide-brimmed hat, take up my special bucket (in which I've punched holes in the bottom to let the water run out when I rinse my catch in the brine), slip on my zoris, and skip over the beach to the sea. (Skip? At my age? With no one to see me, why not?) Soon I'm so adept at finding them that I can pick my favorite spots—a weedy inlet off South Beach at the low-tide line, an ancient lobster buoy at the base of the Shmoos, a certain protected pool high enough on the rocks to remain accessible late on the rising tide, which I reserve for emergencies. Each colony has a slightly different character—like clubs and teams, like villages and towns. I know where there are dark mussels with luminescent inner shells, great reddish-brown horse mussels to chop for chowder, perfect clean blues to decorate a paella; I have a bed of tenacious hangers-on I seek when I want a workout, and a pool of easy pickings to encourage beginners. Even within a single bed, mussels are sometimes so distinctive that I can identify them as they come out of the steaming pot. Their lives are written all over their shells in their size, weight, color, shape, cicatrices, texture, beards, and even in their flesh, which varies in color from deep purple to crimson, from bright orange to vermilion. Some taste salty, some mild. Some are plump, some stunted. I study and eat them all. What once seemed impossible is now a cinch as I follow my nose to the edge of the water, peer into the pools, part the seaweed, feel under the rocks, and score.

I thought I could go along forever following the tides without a thought to the world. Then one June day, finding myself down to my last two onions and a lone potato, without bread, lettuce, or fruit, I fear there is nothing for it but to compile a list, take the shopping cart down from its peg, and walk across the island to the store.

How strange to emerge from my solitude. After weeks with no more human contact than a few words with passing strangers, I'm glad the morning is foggy, with only a couple of lobster boats on the water and not a soul on the beach.

When I reach the store, the cupboard is bare. Supplies have been pretty much cleaned out over the weekend: no lettuce or fruit in the cooler, only one stale loaf of airy bread, and cans as sparse on the shelves as endangered species. The next delivery of bread isn't till Wednesday, of vegetables till Thursday or Friday; I'll just have to come back. I collect some basic items—pasta, sugar, flour, vinegar, oil—plus a box of yeast as backup, then sign the tab and depart.

Back on the beach near the nubble, I notice a patch of lamb's-quarters growing in my path. Lamb's-quarters is the common name of an edible beach plant with small, roughly triangular succulent leaves, deep green on top and silvery on the underside, much like the common edible pigweed. For years I'd been adding a few lamb's-quarters or sorrel leaves to my nubble salads for color whenever I happened to think of it; now, lacking lettuce, I stoop to pick enough for an entire salad.

Filling up my hat, I begin to see how unnecessary it is to go all the way to the store for questionable lettuce when there's plenty of lamb's-quarters that will do. If I can subsist on mussels in place of meat, why not these greens in place of lettuce? Like breast milk, the local fare is easier to come by, fresher, and probably more reliable.

When my hat brims green, I turn to inspect the long low hedge of beach grasses on the neck of sand that separates South Beach from Singing Sand Beach and for the first time wonder if some of them may not also be edible. Up on the bluff too: plenty of sorrel and raspberries grow in the dense brush around the cabin—what else might be there?

On the nature shelf are two books describing wild food by the famous forager Euell Gibbons: the classic *Stalking the Wild Asparagus*, which covers vegetables and fruits, and its companion, *Stalking the Blue-Eyed Scallop*, which describes the trove of edible sea creatures that inhabit the shore. An old birthday gift from Jerry, the *Stalking* books, part cookbooks, part field guides, have for years sat silently among field guides to shells, shorebirds, mushrooms, wildflowers, and stars. I regarded them as reference works to be consulted on specific questions, and though I occasionally looked something up in each volume, I never sat down to read them through, much less go hunting for their treasures. We never stayed long enough to learn even such basic facts about nubble food as that apples from our tree, always small, sour, and bitter-skinned in summer, ripen to large sweet yellow fruit late in fall. If now and then I baked a pie from our green apples, tossed a few wild leaves into the salad, sent the children off with plastic pails to pick raspberries, it was only a moment's glance, like a dash through the Louvre for a glimpse of the Mona Lisa and then goodbye. Among our guests were usually some too squeamish to eat even lamb's-quarters or mussels, much less the more outlandish dandelions, crabs, periwinkles, or sea urchins Gibbons suggests. In a restaurant or from a store, perhaps—recently at Balducci's in Greenwich Village I saw the similar "Lamb's Lettuce," proclaimed "the world's most elegant and delicate salad ingredient," priced at thirty-six dollars a pound—but not when the greens grow raggedly around you like weeds and the shellfish lie in wait ready to squirt, pinch, or flee. Most islanders, fishermen included, disdain the plentiful mussels, and while some may pick blueberries and raspberries, they find the more esoteric berries and greens suspect or worse.

Now, all at once, Gibbons's books seem to offer secrets that I need to know. Though there's no guarantee I can find any of the treasures he describes, I'm avid to try. As soon as I put away the groceries and dress my salad, I pull both volumes down from the shelf, carry them to the table, and begin to read.

How does one go from a picture, a model, a map, or a name into the world? Nothing alive looks much like a picture of it unless you know it already. For the next several days I do nothing but study the text and pore over the line drawings in the books, marking in the margins what looks promising; but as soon as I walk outside I see the same jumble of plants—some vaguely familiar, most as good as invisible—that I've always seen. To read up on a creature and then step outside and find it is about as easy as learning a language by sampling a dictionary. I don't know how to begin to look, and Gibbons, whose drawings are all in black and white, doesn't exactly tell me. What he does instead is something magical: he inspires the precise mix of humility and confidence I need to find them on my own—the humility to accept my ignorance, and the confidence that the task can be done at all.

Whatever his magic, it works, because soon every venture outdoors, even to the outhouse, is a field trip, and every tabletop and counter in the cabin fills up with leaves, berries, seaweeds, and shells. With Gibbons to guide me, I examine them one by one, and my salads grow increasingly complex. For basic lettuce, "wild spinach" composed of lamb's-quarters, orach, strawberry goosefoot; for tartness, sorrel and yellow dock; for a slightly bitter tang, dandelion and mustard leaves; for a strong celery-like flavor, angelica or Scotch lovage; for a radishy bite, sea rocket and the small yellow four-petaled charlock flowers. And that's only a beginning.

•

One afternoon as I walk toward the kitchen to switch on the five o'clock news I become dimly conscious of something unusual at the periphery of my senses. An unfamiliar blur of light, like a snowstorm at dusk. I glance out the windows to see sea gulls, gray, mottled, and white, gliding slowly past the deck toward the near beach and rocky point, converging from all directions.

I've often seen gulls congregate en masse on Obed's Rock, crying raucously by the hundreds at dawn or dusk, but never before on so near a shore. There are dozens of them, then many dozens—calling in the air, circling down, leaning forward with yellow beaks open or stretching their necks toward the sky to wail from the rocks. A few are diving into the water and surfacing with something in their beaks, which they drop on the beach and guard from the approach of other gulls. Through a light fog I see them spread along the beach at intervals like sentries, while the rest mass on the point.

Quickly, I get the binoculars.

Fish! The gulls are catching fish! A large gull will swoop down to pluck a fish out of the water, drop it flopping onto the beach, peck at it until it stops moving, then rip off a chunk and swallow it before another gull running up from behind can snatch it away.

This is something entirely new to me (except for the time Abbie Hoffman, in an effort to mock the bourgeoisie, stood on the visitors' balcony of the New York Stock Exchange and gleefully threw hundreds of dollar bills down onto the floor of the Exchange where mayhem broke out as brokers and clerks scurried after them). I grab my bucket and fly to the beach.

Large silver fish, weighing two, three, even four pounds, dot the beach—most slightly wounded, with blood dulling their silver scales, but leaping still, each one guarded by a gull or two: scavengers turned sentinels. Observing my steady progress, the gulls, so willing to fight each other, shrink back as I approach, abandoning their prey to me. Thrilled at such booty, I see no reason to leave all these fish to the gulls, who don't hesitate to rip off one another. While the gulls look on, I select a few of the larger, livelier fish and drop them into my bucket.

What is a scavenger? One who cleans up someone else's garbage; now that the world is strewn with glut, a benevolent citizen.

In the midst of my collecting, a noisy ATV comes zooming across the beach, scattering the gulls. On it is Mat Burns, my husband's college roommate, who introduced us to this island in the first place and built us our cabin nearly two decades ago. He's the first islander I ever met, and now he's caught me in this most peculiar pursuit. Shall I be embarrassed?

He pulls up and stops. "Whatcha got there in that bucket?"

Excitedly I show him my catch.

"Mackerel," he pronounces. "Real good-sized ones, too. Where'd they come from?"

"The gulls are bringing them in," I announce, expecting Mat to provide an explanation for this amazing event. But he's as puzzled as I am. He looks around and shakes his head, muttering incredulity as he praises the size and beauty of the mackerel, then orders me to bring him a sharp knife.

Obediently I take the stairs two at a time and select a knife from the cabin. When I hand it over, Mat cleans the fish on a flat rock, scaling, beheading, and gutting them with smooth, easy strokes. I watch him closely; I've never cleaned a fish. As he tosses the heads and entrails into the water, gulls swoop down to retrieve them—consolation prizes for the fish I've filched from them.

"Tell you what," says Mat. "Bring them on up to my house and we'll grill them for supper. I've got some people coming and a few lobsters, but we can start off with these." He rubs the knife in the sand, rinses it in the saltwater, and hands it back to me.

An hour later reluctantly I carry the fish up to Mat's house, recalling the first time I crossed this white-sand beach more than twenty years before. "Where the hell are you?" Jerry (not yet my husband) had written to Mat after seeing his name in an alumni magazine. "I'm right here where I belong, on Shark Cove in Casco Bay. Bring a sleeping bag and come see us, you old bastard," Mat had written back. I'd seen the coasts of Italy and France, but never of New England. After a hard drive across five states, Portland looked like the end of the earth to me—a depressed city from another century in the poorest state in the North, with a crumbling waterfront, ramshackle houses, declining population—nothing like the manicured boomtown it became in the Eighties. On the ferry to Long Island, fifty minutes out across Portland Harbor, Jerry and I crept below-decks to escape the wind and tried to listen in on unfathomable conversations of fishermen in slickers, women in parkas and rubber boots, craggy leather-skinned people speaking an unfamiliar dialect.

By the time we reached the island, dusk was falling and a thick fog had rolled in. Behind the pier on the main road were several neat wooden houses and a few dilapidated ones, some rusty antiquated cars missing vital parts, a diner, a church (The Star of the Sea), and a general store, where we asked directions to Mat Burns's house. Through heavy mist we trudged up an asphalt road on a steep hill across the island, down a long dirt road flanked by woods, to the very edge of the sea. Between the night and the fog we could barely see the water, though we heard it pounding the rocks and swashing against the sand, and sometimes felt it nip at our feet. We took off our sandals and hugged the shore, picking our way by flashlight along the long wrack-strewn strand, narrowed by high tide.

After nearly an hour, a half-built cabin and a large tent loomed out of the fog. "Mat?" called Jerry, knocking on the door. A smiling blond woman holding a can of beer opened to us. "Excuse me," said Jerry politely, "is this where Mat Burns lives?"

"You made it! Son of a bitch!" A big ruddy-faced man behind the woman slapped his thigh and handed Jerry a beer. "Goddam if you didn't make it after all! Sally! Take their coats."

Sally hung our coats on nails while Mat, grinning deep creases into his already weather-beaten face, though he couldn't have been much over thirty, led us to a round table (a wooden industrial spool) in the center of the low-ceilinged room heavy with tobacco smoke, where two more men seated on canvas camp chairs looked up from their beers. "Son of a bitch!" repeated Mat, slapping down into his chair. Wide-open face, even teeth, mischievous eyes, square jaw, muscular shoulders, big hands, and that booming, clipped Maine speech.

The room was lit by a single kerosene hurricane lamp in the center of the table and a few candles. After my eyes adjusted to the light, I saw the blond heads of two small boys, a dog, and two cats asleep together on folding cots behind a Franklin stove. I took in the rough rafters, unplastered walls, simple furnishings consisting of the stove, a slate sink, makeshift desk of pine boards resting on orange crates filled with books, and, in the corners, strange wooden shapes I eventually learned were lobster buoys. Drawings torn from a sketch pad were tacked to the plank walls, a straw rug partially covered the floor. Mat, winsome, handsome, pipe-smoking paterfamilias, introduced us to the fishermen at the table. All well looped (it was already past nine: how long we'd been traveling!), the men continued trading stories: the night the herring began to run after a two-week wait; crabs fouling up the nets; the ones that got away.

While I listened, Sally ladled chowder into chipped bowls from a blackened iron pot and handed them around, followed by mugs of boiled coffee and homemade apple pie. My eyes turned and turned, taking in the exotic setting, the unfamiliar people. All my metaphors for Maine, this hitherto unimagined place, came from nineteenth-century boys' novels: kerosene lamps, fishermen, the steady pounding of surf. I might as well have been in Antarctica.

By the time Jerry and I were huddled together in sleeping bags on the beach, the fog had lifted and the tide had receded to reveal a vast expanse of pristine white sand. The stars seemed brighter and more numerous than I had ever seen them before. After a while, Jerry pointed out the aurora borealis, the northern lights. "Where?" I asked, straining to follow his finger. "See? There," he said—so calmly that for years I presumed this wonder of nature to be a common Maine sight, even though I saw it rarely. Finally I began to make it out. Luminous rays stretching downward toward the horizon like the long glinting fingers of myriad hands. The northern lights! I remembered debarking from a student ship in Bremerhaven, Germany, after six days on the ocean, and catching my first sight of a foreign land: the wonder of herring stands and feather beds. Once again, I felt like a foreigner in a strange new country—where this time, however, to my relief the people happened to speak English.

Not long after that, Jerry and I were married; and when our children were toddlers, at Mat's urging and over my veto, we bought the nubble across the beach from his cabin for the absurdly low price of the unpaid taxes.

THE fire's perfect when I arrive at Mat's vastly expanded house. Now deeply creased but with all his old vitality, Mat takes the fish from me and lays them on the grill. Less than two hours out of the water, the mackerel are so tasty, firm, and sweet that the party fails to do justice to King Lobster.

Among the guests at Mat's table I'm amazed to see one of the same fishermen I met that first time here decades before; in place of Sally, though, Mat has a different, a dark-haired, wife, named Patty; and all the children are grown up. How the fish stories fly, circling around the new event. One man recalls how, a few years back, a million dead pogies stank up a town up the coast for an entire week after a school of bluefish in a feeding frenzy chased the bait fish into the marina where they completely clogged the waters and soon suffocated from lack of oxygen. Another recalls that about fifteen years before, on this very island, a school of bluefish ambushed a school of mackerel between Shark Cove and the open sea. The mackerel, attacked and wounded by the predatory blues, fled by the hundreds toward the beach where they were easy prey for the gulls, ever excited by the sight and smell of blood. He wonders if this isn't a repeat.

And sure enough, after dinner when we all walk down to the cove to check the action, we see hovering under the water a small distance from shore the big sinister blues. By the next day it's official: all around the island there's been a mackerel bonanza.

With gulls doing my fishing for me, I'm able to add fish to my growing inventory of food available simply for the taking.

It's the middle of June and hot. I'm out on the beach picking my salad greens leaf by leaf, engrossed in their minute differences, when I become aware of two girls, around seven or eight, following me with their eyes. I'm suddenly self-conscious: how must I look to them in my tattered hat, my mismatched sneakers, a shrunken and faded old anarchist T-shirt ("Question Authority"), carrying a child's pail for a receptacle?

At last one of the girls, her hair in pigtails, approaches me and asks, "Whatcha pickin?" while the other, stringy black hair falling in her eyes, hangs slightly back.

"It's orach," I explain. "I use it for salad. And this is strawberry goosefoot. Want a taste?"

Hesitating, noncommittal—"You *eat* it?"

"Sure." I pop a leaf into my mouth to demonstrate, then hold one out to her. "It's good. Try it."

But she takes a tiny step backward; and seeing the skeptical, hesitant faces, I realize that their parents must often have warned them not to eat anything unknown and never to accept gifts from strangers. I smile, shrug, continue to collect my greens.

Before long the other child, the dark-haired one still hanging back, asks, "Don't you ever get sick?"

"Oh, no. I only eat the plants I know."

"How do you know?"

"I study them. I have books about them. I'm very careful, really." And indeed, I do subject each new species I find to a set of stringent tests. First I check my reference books till I'm reasonably confident of what I have. Then I taste a small specimen, closely observing its flavor, smell, texture, and bite before spitting it out. My first actual swallow I limit to a tiny morsel; a day later I try a slightly larger sample; and only after a third sampling with no adverse reaction do I admit the candidate to my repertory.

"Do strawberries really grow here?" asks the bolder, pigtailed girl.

"Not strawberries; strawberry goosefoot, named for its tiny red fruit." I wonder: have they never seen strawberries growing? But of course, you don't know till you know. And then I remember my own astonishment the first time I saw, at the Union Square Market, the way brussels sprouts sprout from their stalk, dozens of them spiraling in a helix pattern around a straight fat arm.

The girls follow close behind me, asking questions until my pail is full and I'm ready to leave. "See you around," they shout, as if my sneakers matched.

The next day when they come to the beach they're accompanied by a woman—their mother, I presume. I wave, and they, like the polite girls they are, wave back, but without glancing at the greens they're crossing through. They proceed on down to the water's edge and spread towels. Every so often, when she thinks I won't notice, I catch the woman looking my way, trying, I suppose, to assess the danger—and I remember the hermit I visited on the backside of Tahiti back in the early Sixties.

I'd read about those odd Frenchmen who gave up Paris for—what? A rough hut, breadfruit, bananas, no one to talk to. I'd been told they were hostile and suspicious behind their walls, would hide if you came near. But when, unable to contain my curiosity, I gingerly approached the hut where one of them lived, he greeted me eagerly, begged a cigarette, and insisted I sit on a crude bench in his yard, where he sat beside me, greedily soliciting news.

I pitied him. His large head looked ancient with its thin white hair, grizzly beard, hooked nose, red eyes, leathery skin. He wore homemade sandals and a sarong that fell from his waist to his bony knees. His yard was strewn with odd implements—coconut husks, seashells, fishing nets, a small upturned boat. When I had answered some of his questions, he began to answer mine, describing his life, its pros and cons. On one side, ease and simplicity; on the other, loneliness and endless feuds with the government. Bitterly he spewed forth his critique of Paris, France, "civilization." As we talked, his quick fingers wove palm fronds into thatch like the roof of his hut.

Ignorant that France was developing Tahiti as a nuclear base and using that part of the Pacific as a testing site, I presumed that his contempt for France was sour grapes. His bitterness, combined with his unexpected openness with an English-speaking stranger, I interpreted to mean that he regretted trading his former world for some unachievable dream, and I dismissed him as a colorful self-deluded crank unwilling to admit he had made a mistake, perhaps even a fraud.

Now I know the mistake was mine, not his. Mine for judging his consciously invented life by my naïve, conventional one, for presuming to interpret his life rather than accepting his interpretation. As I begin to uncover a whole new world myself, I see the folly of that snap judgment. When people approach me on the beach to see what I'm picking and ask me what I've got in my bucket, I sometimes see in their eyes the same embarrassed mix of curiosity, suspicion, and disdain I felt toward that Tahitian hermit. I see them pity me—strange, besneakered lady hermit—wondering how I stay alive and why I want to. But as I slip a leaf of orach in my mouth, tasty, pesticide-free, richer in Vitamin A than spinach, I remember my own ignorant presumption and laugh.

It takes only a couple of weeks before my basic island diet consists of local species of wild vegetables, fruits, and shellfish—and I've barely made a dent in Gibbons. I've learned to focus the blur by slowing way down and turning all my attention to what's right there in front of me: this leaf, this seed, this crab. At a glance I'm able to tell the difference now between charlock and yellow dock, between raspberry and blackberry canes, between tender periwinkles and tougher whelks, and I'm getting ready to take on seaweeds. Though at first each distinction seems impossible, each new quarry unattainable, eventually the moment comes when it's mine forever, as a word you can use correctly becomes part of your permanent vocabulary. Every day, circling the nubble with my pail, I rejoice in my riches, feeling doubly blessed: once for the miracle of knowledge and again for the miracle of food. A new world, close as my body and old as the sea, has opened up to me. These found meals—absorbing to assemble, nutritiously balanced, lavishly varied, and virtually free—are as delicious and healthy as any I've ever eaten. An initiate, I celebrate with each knowing bite sacramental transformations: from a crab scuttling in the cove or a pea fattening in a pod in the morning to blood coursing through my veins come night; even the excess flowing through my body into the privy down to the earth comes back to life again. I, who had been such a stranger to prayer that my response to grace at table was always embarrassment, now find heating my juices, welling up in my saliva, spiking my tastebuds, stimulating my heartbeat, spicing each delicious mouthful that rich emotional stew of awe, gratitude, and delight that must have prompted the first blessing of food. Hardly by design or even desire, I soon discover I can no longer eat without grace on my lips.

THREE

THE surf recedes, the waters roll back, and I find myself in a new world. Last night there was a full moon, and now the sea is so low that for several hours around the turning of the ebb tide the white beach of Shark Cove sports a black weedy fringe at the water's edge, and a wide bar briefly connects South Beach with Marsh Island—as, I suppose, the waters of the Red Sea parted before Moses. Since the tides are the ocean's response to the pull of the moon and the sun, the height of the tide varies as the moon waxes and wanes. And just as the moon rises later each night, so the high tides are correspondingly later. Twice each lunar month, at the new moon and the full moon, the high flood tides are at their highest and the low ebb tides at their lowest; in the months around the solstices, when moon and sun are lined up with Earth so as to exert their maximum gravitational pull, the flood tides rise so high on the beach that the neck of the nubble all but disappears underwater, leaving this spit of land an island off an island, and the ebb tides recede so far from shore that I can walk all the way to Marsh Island and back on the rocky bar without getting caught by the returning tide. Now seaweeds and shellfish undreamed of by the occasional bather or boater sailing above are briefly exposed: purple sea urchins with their delicate yellow roe, great pink starfish, the rare spiraled moon shell, enormous crabs and mussels, even young lobsters that once I actually caught with my bare hands.

"The shore has a dual nature, changing with the swing of the tides, belonging now to the land, now to the sea. . . . Only the most hardy and adaptable can survive in a region so mutable," writes Rachel Carson in *The Edge of the Sea.* It seems that I, inflexible urbanite, have joined the hardy and adaptable.

Always before a creature of others—of Jerry, the family, the world—I'd expected solitude to be the challenge, the handicap, the price to pay for the freedom to feel and think unencumbered. For while part of me always longed for it —the part that had angled for a single in the dorm, rejoiced when my husband was called out of town, and occasionally sent me off to an artists' colony—another part cowered before the loneliness and anxiety that threatened to follow freedom, the part that made me marry at twenty and that kept me married, ostensibly for the children's sake, after love died. In the ceaseless battle between the two my fears won out, sending me dashing to safety after each tentative charge on freedom.

But now I find that solitude, far from being the price, is turning out to be the prize. Solitude its own reward! Instead of making me anxious, it seems to be sweeping away my anxieties, opening up possibilities, and as I walk from cabin to rocks to beach to cove to outhouse and shed and back again, I feel a composure I've never known before. At night I fall into bed weary instead of tense. My fingernails, bitten since childhood, are growing long. Not that I've willed them to grow—years of trying haven't worked; I simply notice, one day after clamming, an irritating deposit of grit beneath ten unfamiliar growths on my hands. Just so, after half a lifetime of adapting to the needs of others in the high tide of the family, here at fifty, with no one to ask or answer to, I'm beginning to see who I am when the tide goes out.

KNEELING before the Franklin stove and crumpling paper to start a fire, I reach into the pile of old newspapers and pull out an obscure literary journal. It's six years old, I may have read it; shall I burn it? I look over the contents page. The essays look mildly interesting; I wonder who brought it here and why. A couple of poems catch my eye. I put it aside and crumple something else, noting that a year ago I'd most likely have burned the journal as dated. But old habits are losing their hold on me.

For years I avidly read books and eagerly wrote them, systematically trying to stuff my head with all the thoughts of mankind, but always so determined to master a subject or pursue a goal that I seldom practiced the simple pleasures of reading whatever caught my fancy or following a thought wherever it happened to lead. My plans and projects were usually so backed up that no matter what work I was engaged in at any moment, I suspected it ought to be something else. Once, I started a short story in which the protagonist leaves home for a month in order to devote herself to completing a story she's been writing, but she slips away from her place of refuge to another retreat to begin a different one, and from that one she plays hooky for yet another one. Each time she leaves one undertaking to pursue another, she leaves a bit of herself behind, until by the time she steals back to her starting place she is strung out with no stories left at all. I never finished the story.

Now, evidently, a tide has turned. Without a witness, what I ought to do and what I want to do begin to merge, until I lose my ability to distinguish them. My ambitious ego-driven will, that muscular taskmaster I've cultivated for years and honored with obedience, ambles languidly in the sun, awaiting my orders. Instead of leading, it seems content to follow along wherever I want to go: down to the shore with a bucket, into the kitchen with a specimen, curled up before the fire with an unexpected book—not one of the books I sent on ahead from my other life but, like my new food and my old clothes, one I find here waiting.

When the fire's crackling, I meander freely among the books as I last did as a child loose in the library. The old literary journal on the kindling pile is as satisfying as the newest ones creating a stir back in the city. The fat college anthologies of world literature I once picked up at St. Joseph the Provider but never found time to read, the odd assortment of paperbacks left behind by visitors seem as brilliant as the stars—the very stars obscured in the city by artificial light. I know that any book or magazine in print can be had through mail order or subscription, but *making do* seems more appealing than *keeping up*. Here in the college readers are thousands of pages packed with works by writers I've been meaning to read for years, mixed with some I've never heard of. Here are the Bible and Baldwin, Le Guin and Lessing, Blake, Whitman, Dickinson, Mann, Castaneda, Kafka, Stravinsky, Tolstoy, the Brontës—

Ever since the early Fifties in New York, when I first read the Brontës as I rode the subway between upper Broadway, where I lived, and my Wall Street clerical job, I've wanted to reread them. But too much else was lined up waiting; rereading was a luxury I had no time for. But now time has stepped out of its running shoes, dropped its disguises, returned to the rhythm of the tides, the cycles of the planets and the moon, the slow ripening of the plants I gather, the long leavening of the yeasty breads I bake. Pointless to try to slow or hurry it, much less to "save" it. Slowly the kneaded dough rises in the bowl at its own pace, and after the first long rising you punch it down and let it rise again, and when it once more fills the pan, you bake it. The rich aroma of freshly baked bread permeates the cabin all day long, and each time you cut a slice, spread it with jam, chew it, you experience again the whole sensuous process: the kneading, the rising, the punching down, the baking. Gradually I realize that the very concept *saving time* is either a solecism (surely time goes at its own good pace) or a waste (save it for what?); the more lavishly I spend time, the more I seem to have, like the wild leaves I pluck for salad which grow more lushly the more I pick. In nubble time history melts away, taking with it all traces of the number game. Old, young, obsolete—these time-bounded words don't apply in a realm where there's time enough for everything; indeed, all the time in the world.

"THINK long thoughts," I read in a strange book with a fuchsia cover. The author is P. D. Ouspensky, a follower of Gurdjieff, both early-twentieth-century Russian-born mystics. "Each of our thoughts is too short. Until you have experience from your own observation of the difference between long and short thoughts, this idea will mean nothing to you."

Until this moment, I've been one to whom the idea of a long thought meant nothing; it never even crossed my mind. I lay the book in my lap and reflect: have I experienced the difference between long and short thoughts or haven't I? Perhaps not before this summer, never having been alone long enough. But recently I do seem to have had the luxury of several rather long, uninterrupted, exhilarating thoughts—though maybe not long enough to qualify. How long is long? And long enough for what? I'm puzzled, intrigued; the question certainly seems worth investigating.

Here I must confess that before coming alone to the nubble I would never have had a moment for a book by a mystic, particularly one that called itself *Conscience: The Search for Truth.* Having come of age in the Fifties, a time when the very concept of Truth with a capital T was suspect, when the fashionable philosophical theory logical positivism held that nothing can be known except what can be stated in verifiable sentences, I would have dismissed such a book with a snicker. But here on the nubble, where no one can judge my thoughts, and snickers have nothing to feed on, I'm free to read anything I like. Indeed, now that I'm following my nose, whatever I read seems like a special message beamed directly to me. Just as the most innocuous-looking plants are gifts of sustenance, so even the most unlikely authors speak to me. Is this what it means to be in tune with your surroundings?

Looking out over the sea I recall an earlier time when I had been briefly but intensely curious about matters mystical. It had begun with a strange episode on a speeding subway train.

I was sitting alone on the downtown IRT on my way to pick up the children at their after-school music classes. The train had just pulled out of the Twenty-third Street station and was accelerating to its cruising speed. All around me people sat bundled up in mufflers, damp woolen coats, and slush-stained boots, reading newspapers or staring off blankly as the train jerked along the track. The air was cold and close, with the smell of stale tobacco clinging to winter coats. An elderly pair exchanged words in a Slavic tongue; a mother read an advertising sign to her three bedraggled, open-mouthed children.

Then suddenly the dull light in the car began to shine with exceptional lucidity until everything around me was glowing with an indescribable aura, and I saw in the row of motley passengers opposite the miraculous connection of all living beings. Not felt; saw. What began as a desultory thought grew to a vision, large and unifying, in which all the people in the car hurtling downtown together, including myself, like all the people on the planet hurtling together around the sun—our entire living cohort—formed one united family, indissolubly connected by the rare and mysterious accident of life. No matter what our countless superficial differences, we were equal, we were one, by virtue of simply being alive at this moment out of all the possible moments stretching endlessly back and ahead. The vision filled me with overwhelming love for the entire human race and a feeling that no matter how incomplete or damaged our lives, we were surpassingly lucky to be alive. Then the train pulled into the station and I got off.

I emerged from the subway stunned and thrilled. Crisp midday light glinted off the windows of a tall apartment building across the street; a high wind shivered through me and shook the corner traffic lights. I looked around at the familiar world, which was the same yet not the same. My ordinary existence had been shattered, letting me glimpse something I had never before imagined, something I could not begin to describe.

If only I could see it again! But I had no idea how to get it back. It had come and gone unbidden, without the least boost (or hindrance) from my will. It was as if I had suddenly fallen through a deep hole into another world only to emerge again as suddenly. Besides, if I didn't hurry I'd be late for the children.

In order to keep it alive, at least prevent the memory from fading too quickly, I needed to speak of my experience. But whom could I tell? Who would care to believe me? No one I knew. In my Manhattan, mysticism was scorned; mystics, like Communists, and the few bookstores that catered to either, were underground. Still, I could not doubt that my vision had occurred, even though I had no way to verify it. And this inspired in me a new humility toward such knowledge and a secret gratitude that the vision had appeared to me, an atheistically tending agnostic.

Time passed, and though I would not forget or deny my strange experience, it made me so uncomfortable that it ossified into a mere biographical fact, something slightly embarrassing that had once unaccountably happened to me.

Alone on the nubble, I'm now able to recall that momentous event of decades before without embarrassment. Mixing it with water, wind, and memory, I reconstitute the desiccated fact as a full-blown experience pulsing with life. The vision of unity I saw on that subway begins here to extend beyond humanity to the whole natural world. No longer is it tainted as *mystic*, for here, with no one passing judgment, no experience is tainted. The effort of thought is always the effort to see underlying patterns; here with no distractions—or rather, where nothing I do can distract me from my thought—the patterns and hidden harmonies begin to dance before me. Perhaps I'll have all the time I need to follow a thought, any thought, wherever it leads for as long as it takes to come to clarity.

It's Saturday, and I'm walking home from "down front" where I've just stopped at the store, the post office, and the pay phone to make my weekly calls to my family. At the crest of the hill I stop short as I read an alarmed note from my old friend Katherine: "We worry about you up there by yourself. It's not healthy to be so much alone. Isn't it time for you to come back home?"

I'm shocked. I'd written her five pages about my love affair with solitude and how grateful I feel to be living on this island, but instead of rejoicing she's distressed, afraid I may be flipping out. She's one of my closest friends, one of the eight feminists with whom I'd been meeting once a week for years to try to keep alive the passion we first developed in the late Sixties when the movement known as the Second Wave of feminism stormed the historical stage, giving us the role of our lives. Now, years later, when so many women have grown weary, discouraged, or distracted, we still try to carry on with our protests and actions, fighting injustice as we did back when the movement was young, vigorous, and winning.

I fold up the letter and stop to pick serviceberries, or pie berries, my newest find, off three high bushes along the road. For weeks I've been eyeing these small smooth-skinned spheres that resemble huckleberries and have ripened to a dull red; though bland and tasteless when raw, they are reputedly delicious in a pie. Thinking about Katherine's letter as I fill my sack, I'm not exactly sure myself what to make of the changes I'm undergoing. But far from flipping out, I feel whole, the opposite of crazy. The anxieties I suffered only months ago over the state of the world and the weight of my years have fallen away, replaced in this tranquil space by acceptance of what I find, of who I am. *Amor fati* goes the Latin proverb now tacked up over my desk: accept what is—literally, love fate.

Perhaps I shouldn't have tried to explain to Katherine what I'm feeling here. What friend wants to know that you prefer to be alone? Even my children seem suspicious of this move away, as if it means I care about them less, despite how eagerly I anticipate our Saturday talks or how disappointed I am if they're out when I call. Katherine seems worried, as I sometimes am myself, that solitude is eroding the passion from my politics, as if harmony and struggle are two masters that cannot both be served. After all, it's hard to be an activist by yourself—particularly in a movement that exalts community and distrusts all individualists and loners.

I think wistfully back to those idealistic days in the movement when we made all decisions by consensus, rotating tasks or choosing them by lot so that each of us could be empowered. We learned to listen hard and think together, insisting at each meeting that everyone speak her mind. We studied oratory, self-defense, anatomy, electricity, car repair, carpentry, history—imagining we could make ourselves so strong and skilled that we could each take responsibility for everything in our lives. Maybe, I think, I've come to a place where I can again expand my powers and live once more by consensus—but this time consensus of one.

Back in the cabin I mix the berries with sugar and lemon peel, then roll out the pie crusts. The hand method of doing things is making me stronger every day. Extensions of my hands, my tools are teaching me artistry I never knew myself capable of. In my kitchen, equipped mainly with discards from an army of kitchen modernizers, I can perform every desired task; I am three generations behind and probably as many ahead as I cut my pastry with a wooden-handled wire pastry blender, beat batter with a wooden spoon, strain the peels from my applesauce or mash potatoes in a hand-powered food mill, grind seeds with a mortar and pestle, whip egg whites with a whisk, grate against a versatile hand grater, juice on a ridged glass juicer, toast on a four-sided toaster set over an open flame, sweep with a broom, and brew in a drip pot the coffee I grind by turning a handle and feeling each bean crumble as the gears bite down.

While the pie bakes, I pick up the freshman reader and open to a luminous essay by James Baldwin, "Notes of a Native Son." His thoughts surround and carry me until, as

I reach the final page, I find myself immersed in the fundamental political question, the disturbing paradox awakened in me by Katherine's letter. "It began to seem," writes Baldwin,

> that one would have to hold in the mind forever two ideas which seemed to be in opposition. The first idea was acceptance, the acceptance totally without rancor, of life as it is, and men as they are: in the light of this idea, it goes without saying that injustice is a commonplace. But this did not mean that one could be complacent, for the second idea was of equal power: that one must never, in one's own life, accept these injustices as commonplace but must fight them with all one's strength.

But how, I wonder, laying down the book. How can it be done? How hold in the mind for a moment—much less forever, as Baldwin commands—ideas and feelings so locked in opposition as acceptance and resistance, contemplation and struggle, solitude and solidarity, harmony and political passion? How can one live without rancor in a world steeped in suffering and injustice—or live without contentment in a world bathed in birdsong at sundown?

All through dinner Baldwin's paradox nags at me. I continue to chew on it even as I taste my first bite ever of serviceberry pie—which I have to concede is disappointing: a bit mealy and bland, like the dried blueberries in a box of muffin mix. It pesters me until, after I brush my purple-tinted teeth at the edge of the deck and light the evening lamp, I take up my reading again.

And now I'm forced to confront the conflict from another side, this time by Jacobo Timerman, an Argentine newspaper editor who was imprisoned and tortured for his politics. Reading his ironic reflection on how his particular mix of views utterly baffled his captors, slowly I begin to understand that no one's life can make perfect sense to another person.

> Colonel Battesti wanted . . . Timerman . . . to explain what he was doing in the Youth League for Freedom, why he was supporting that strange alliance between the United States and Russia, why he was active in Zionism and simultaneously reading Freud and fighting against Perón, and was also a Socialist though claiming to be opposed to Russian totalitarianism. . . . This was the same individual who, according to the police report, had given a lecture at the age of twenty or twenty-two at the Academy of Plastic Arts, formulating a proposal in support of cubism, structuralism, constructivism, or some other ism. . . . They couldn't accept or comprehend that an Argentine patriot could simultaneously be a patriotic Jew, a Zionist of the Left, a publisher of psychology books, a defender of Salvador Allende, of the Soviet dissidents, and of political prisoners in Cuban jails.

Why, I wonder, must my former selves—the committed political activist, the loyal feminist, the passionate mother, the engaged writer—compete with the quiet person I'm becoming here. Why can't all of them reside in me as confidently as Timerman's seemingly dissonant selves reside in him? Doesn't he show that a life, a soul, is spacious enough for everything in it? Isn't it as futile to ask oneself to choose among the impulses that live inside one as to ask the shore to justify its constantly changing appearance?

My colleague S., writing from the Royal Carnival Beach Hotel on a small Caribbean island where she and Jimmy are taking a week's vacation, asks if I too have been "getting in touch with nature." She says she has been swimming laps until her crawl is now under a minute per lap—twenty percent faster than she did the day they arrived. Twenty percent in less than a week!

Is that getting in touch with nature? I suppose so: what in this world is not nature? As, equally, what in this world has not been affected by us? Our fallout falls everywhere, part of nature too. The city is nature; electricity is nature; power, poetry, and pollution are all equally part of nature. Are molecular biology and physical chemistry nature? A three-minute lap or a six-minute egg? If not, then S. herself, with her sleek muscled body and her bleached-blond hair, is not. I don't know if I'm more or less in touch with nature than I was before I came to live here, but I'm certainly more in touch with myself. I want to tell S. I'm getting in touch with the given, inside and out. For example:

Last week I woke up one morning to see a large brown blob at the water's edge. The tide was halfway out. Through the binoculars I thought I made out an animal stretched out on the beach on a beeline from my window.

I ran down to investigate. It was a dead seal with light tan fur, open eyes, and a set of small, even teeth. I poked at its decomposing body with a long driftwood stick, working to turn it over. No visible genitals, but two round holes on either side running clear through the body and connected by gashes, chunks of flesh missing from its back. I tried to shove it off the beach into the water, but it was bloated and heavy and wouldn't roll. Maybe the tide would take it out. "Yeah, sometimes fishermen take shots at the seals when they got nothing to do," said one of the women at the store. Of course!—those were bullet holes. "But," I asked, "then why are there chunks missing?" "Dunno. Maybe sharks got after it," said someone else. "The smell of blood."

When I examined the seal again after returning from the

store, I noticed a perfect set of claws on each of its rather stubby flippers, long dark nails like Joan Crawford's in a black-and-white still. Mammal, I thought. Perfect manicured fingernails, dark and shapely, ladylike.

Before nightfall, the seal had disappeared on the tide, making me sorry not to have taken a nail or two. When it was back again on the far side of the beach the next morning I didn't hesitate. I put on two of the blue cotton fishermen's gloves from the dozen or so I've salvaged from a certain spot on South Beach where they're always washing up (Once I found gloves at that spot for eight days running when I went across for the mail—mostly lefthanded. Where did they come from? Why just there?), took down a pair of pliers, and carefully plied off eight nails, leaving one on each flipper—like the bit of food some people ritually leave on their plate to give something back.

Getting them out was a harder job than I'd expected, but once I began I was determined. Most of the nails wound up with bits of fur still clinging to them; this worried me because there was no knowing how long the seal had been dead or what organisms had invaded it. Sappho wisely warned, "If you're squeamish, don't prod the beach rubble." Here, I've shed my squeamishness. Still wearing gloves, I washed off the nails in seawater, then carried them in a horse-mussel shell up to the cabin, where I sterilized them in boiling water.

If that's getting in touch with nature, I say to S. (alone, I speak to anyone I like), then how come the gloves? But she's hardly one to tell about stripping the claws from a dead seal, and doesn't get my joke. As I arrange the nails on a shelf among shells and bones, I think about S. on her island and I on mine. Are we different or alike? She's out to break records, I to establish mine by discovering how little I need in order to have everything, how much awaits me under the tide, how long I can stretch the season without freezing or cracking. My new rules are few and simple: follow my interest; go as deep as I can; change the rules whenever I like.

For two months my desk remained pristine as on the day I arrived—a tabula rasa of a desk, no files overflowing, no papers covered with my faint script scattered in low piles around the floor or in high piles on the desk, no assortment of notebooks, each an attempt at order, containing lists, and lists of lists. The pile of notes and fragments of manuscript for the book I'd planned to write lay undisturbed on the shelf where I'd first deposited them. If I eyed them now and then it was with forgiveness, as one forgives the debt of a needy friend. As long as the desk was clean and uncluttered everything seemed possible.

But gradually, as I noted down my culinary finds and copied out passages from my readings, my persistent self with its tenacious habits began to leave its traces, until by now the cabin has taken on the inescapable look of all my abodes. The clean desk, fresh notebooks, new files have started to resemble all the desks, notebooks, and files I produce everywhere I go, and the tiny scrawl I can never seem to enlarge, much less escape, spreads through the cabin like invading ants—on the backs of envelopes and scraps of paper, newly started notebooks, a mounting pile of correspondence—until I recognize that the inhabitant of this cabin, for all my transformations, is none other than the inhabitant of this body. Not less my familiar self for being here alone but, without the confines and conflicts of the life I've left behind, the more so. Like the shore changing with the swing of the tides, I seem to be uncovering long-hidden propensities, dormant aspects of myself newly exposed by the pull of the moon. For here I am when the tide goes out—speeder slowing down, fighter finding harmony, activist turned contemplative, analyzer seeking synthesis, communard become solitaire, rationalist grown spiritual, teacher turned student, desirer dissolving in contentment.

I wonder if these uncoverings are the blessings—often seen as the curses—of age? Changes grounded in experience? Whatever they are, here, where time is still, I welcome them. *Amor fati*: love what is. Including my expanding self.

When the August moon begins to wane, I turn again to my manuscript.

FOUR

I WAS nearing the cabin with a bucket of clams in one hand and a giant strand of kelp in another when I tripped and fell on a rock. Somehow, by letting the seaweed go, I managed to break my fall with one hand and prevent my head from cracking; but my torso smacked into the rock, scraping along the sharp barnacles, and the clams flew from the bucket and scattered. I got to my feet and retrieved the clams; and as I cleaned off my bloody body I thought how lucky I was to have escaped with nothing but a skin wound.

That was yesterday; today I'm in pain. As soon as I try to get out of bed, knives start at my side and rip up toward my teeth. I crawl to the aspirin. No help. When I try to lie down again, it's excruciating.

Shall I be afraid? Over the years I've noted how visitors' fears of the solitary life have generally divided by sex. Men fear injury—the broken limb with no one around to care for them—while women, traditionally the caregivers, instead fear the stranger, the hacker. Men fear "nature"; women fear men. Now, with no stranger on the horizon, I follow form, despite the pain.

I soon conclude I've broken a rib. My aged father, who has several times cracked his brittle ribs, once told me there's nothing a doctor can do about them except send you home to heal. Since I'm over fifty myself, I figure mine will probably take some time. Hoping to tame my pain, I study it. Upright I find it's tolerable, but raising or lowering my torso is agony—so I devise a way of sleeping with my back propped against a mound of pillows. I'm okay if I avoid sudden motions and certain specific rotations. Soon my pain is as much a part of me as the calluses on my feet, as familiar as my hands with their blue veins. Whoever I was before, this is who I am now—and managing. Since walking slowly is not unbearable and neither is squatting, I'm able with care to continue gathering my food. Each successful meal reconciles me to the person I've become; instead of damaged I feel accomplished—the opposite of obsolete.

But several weeks later my confidence is tested as, feeling the floor suddenly begin to shake, I look out to see a stranger climbing the stairs. Forgetting myself, I leap up, sending a sharp reminder shooting up my side, and rush onto the deck to meet a man dressed, astonishingly, in jacket and tie.

"Morning," he says, thrusting at me a card identifying him as Ethan Groate, Tax Appraiser. I examine it, then reluctantly invite him in.

Perspiring from his long walk across the sunny beach, though it's already mid-September, Ethan Groate stands dazed for a moment in the center of the room, holding his attaché case. His spare middle-aged frame is topped by a large head with sallow cheeks, thin lips, and receding chin. Blinking behind his glasses, he pulls from his breast pocket a plaid handkerchief, shakes it open, and mops his skinny neck. Then he slowly looks me over before turning his appraising glance to the cabin, which he begins to circle. I watch him take in the open shelves, the cast-iron stoves, the chunky pink piano, the old seaside scenes from St. Joseph the Provider that I've tacked up here and there.

"When was this cottage built—turn of the century?"

I'm amazed that someone in his line of work could be off by more than half a century. "Nineteen sixty-five," I say, pointing to the framed Certificate of Occupancy, and wonder how old he considers me.

He looks from the document to me and around the room, shaking his head. "Nothing much here but the bare studs and rafters," he says to excuse his error, waving at the uninsulated walls and ceiling. He looks at the mess in the kitchen where I've just been peeling a pot of the small sour apples suitable only for cooking that I gathered from under my tree. He pokes his head into the storeroom: tools and towels hang on nails, miscellaneous supplies in empty coffee cans and boxes are piled neatly on deep shelves, and a salvaged bathroom sink stands beneath the window looking past the outhouse far out to Dedgers. Here's where I take my semiweekly sponge baths by the old-fashioned pitcher-and-basin method, using a pot for pitcher and the sink for basin, and when I'm done I let the water run out the drain that empties through a hose out a hole in the wall. On hot days I sometimes dip in the icy ocean or else shower with water heated in the sun in a giant black plastic douche bag called a "sun shower" that I suspend from a hook over the sink. On cold days I may soak my feet in a tub of luxuriously steaming water, my make-do version of a hot tub.

Ethan Groate tries the faucets, but nothing comes. "No plumbing?" he accuses. I shake my head and indicate the outhouse. He opens his attaché case and jabs down a few notations, then closes it and heads out the back door.

From the deck I watch him negotiate the path to the outhouse, his mouth turned down distastefully. He takes a cursory look inside, then hurries back to the cabin. Fixing me with a suspicious stare, he asks, "No septic tank?" I shake my head. "No electricity? No telephone?" I keep on shaking no. "Pretty spartan here, wouldn't you say?"

Spartan? I don't know what to say. This cabin is furnished with everything I could want for my luxurious life and seems anything but spartan. The luxuries I live with are circa 1910—hand pump, gaslights, woodstove—but they're luxuries no less. Still, I'm glad the Tax Appraiser thinks it's spartan, and like a wily merchant consummating a shady deal I readily agree.

He makes some final notes and looking past or through me mutters, "You'll be hearing from us," as his footsteps boom down the stairs.

While I finish the applesauce and clean up the kitchen I try to imagine how this cabin must appear to Ethan Groate. The porcelain surface of the secondhand kitchen sink reveals a network of fine surface cracks distinguishable from dirt only by one who scrubs it. Wiping the long counter, I notice it crumbling near the pump; soon I'll have to replace it. Both cast-iron woodstoves are relics: to use the Franklin stove safely I must frequently mend it with stove cement, and the elegant Queen Atlantic that now serves merely as a countertop has long since rusted out of use. Only one of the burners on the gas stove that replaced it can be turned down to simmer without going out, and the door to the oven won't open all the way. The ancient gas refrigerator sports a screwdriver for a door handle. In the eight storm doors on the long sides of the cabin, two panes have been cracked forever, but I've never thought to replace them since they keep the rain out well enough. The screen inserts have all been patched. The doors themselves need painting. The pink piano, which once boomed out rousing accompaniments for our weekend songfests, has four dysfunctional keys and no more pedal or cutoff. In fact, except for the faded canvas director's chairs and the walnut medicine cabinet I once salvaged from the dump, then stripped, oiled, and reglazed, not a single piece of furniture in the motley collection would be presentable anywhere else. The remnant rugs are unraveling, the wood chests have holes, the desk chair has a loose castor that falls off if you move a certain way, the side tables, consisting of driftwood boards set upon boxes, are tippy, the cots sag. The doors stick when it rains, and water stains—remnants of violent storms that drove the rain in under the doors and around the windows—rise up the raw wood walls and spread out on the floor. Windows don't match, deck boards are loose, and battens are gradually coming unnailed.

A ruin!—as perhaps I too appear to Ethan Groate. Yet, like the unexpected reflection I sometimes catch in a window, which looks more like my aging mother than myself, I've come to cherish it no less. Waking in the early light, I study the long rafters and studs like ribs and bones, the grains of the varied woods like networks of nerves, knots like eyes, arteries of copper tubing that rise from the propane tanks beneath the deck and snake along the rafters and down the walls to each lamp. Listening to the pulse of waves against the shore, I feel the house come alive as each day awakens in song.

Murray Schafer, who tape-recorded the dawn in rural British Columbia, describes the dawn chorus in a book I once found on the beach:

> Following the first bird, the chorus gradually rose in complexity and intensity, peaking after about half an hour, then settled back to sustain itself on a less frenzied level throughout the day. Of special interest to us was the manner in which each species woke up as a group, sang vibrantly for a few moments, then seemed to fall back as another species came forward. The effect is analogous to the different sections of an orchestra entering separately before combining in the total orchestration. I have found

no ornithologist to provide an explanation for this effect, though it is very clear on our recording.

Sometimes I'm startled awake by the thump of heavy gulls landing on the roof, once by a woodpecker hammering on my ear through the bedroom wall, occasionally by barn swallows chattering on the porch railing outside my window. Without insulation, the roof reverberates like a sounding board, a drumskin, a set of strings stretched across the rafters to catch the staccato-clear splatter and plink of each individual drop when it starts to rain, until, as the rain falls harder, the roof gives back a trill, a tremolo, a chord, a roll. And beneath the chorus like a ground bass beats the complicated rhythm of the sea, thundering at high tide or murmuring at low, gentle as brushes or furious as cymbals, as it laps protected Singing Sand Beach to the north, crashes on the rocks of Dedgers to the east, and pounds against South Beach, stretched out along the back of the nubble.

I gather up the apple peels and step out on the deck to toss them, in the direction of the apple tree, down into the dense acre of brush and shrubbery that surrounds the cabin. What would Ethan Groate have to say about this? "No garbage can? No compost heap?" The whole nubble is my compost heap as I fling what little garbage I produce in as wide an arc as I can to join the apples, bay leaves, and rose hips already rotting on the ground.

Beyond Dedgers there's a boat anchored, with two people in wet suits going over the side. Heeding a call of nature, I head for the privy, where I can watch them dive. Back in the days when the cabin was crowded with visitors, this outhouse was my refuge—like the bathroom of my childhood, the one lockable room in the house, the only place where privacy was guaranteed. Architecturally a puppy of the main cabin, identical in its board-and-batten exterior and the low pitch of its roof, the outhouse has two small rooms: one the woodshed, the other the throne room. Except on the rare still summer day, the single hole, freshened by ocean breezes, collects few foul smells, no flies.

Whereas in the city, despite the most lavish bourgeois bathrooms, using the toilet is considered at best indecorous, using this privy is one of the day's most satisfying interludes. (So it must have been in the grand Roman imperial privy, mosaic-adorned, that I once saw in an excavation in Rome, and again in a bathhouse in Pompeii, with holes for perhaps a dozen people to sit and shit together in council; so was it for the Queen in the excavated toilet chamber at the palace of Knossos on the isle of Crete.) From this perfect bird blind of a privy, built on a platform with a protective roof and open front facing the sea, I can watch the swallows feeding their young in the rafters, or follow a marsh hawk glide in low easy loops around the nubble as it hunts field mice. From this pew I have marked the progress of the seasons in the flower-crammed brush: fiddleheads and berry blossoms in early spring, wild roses, nightshade, and touch-me-nots in summer, goldenrod and pale purple asters now, in fall. Knowing I can see them but they can't see me on my shaded seat, I watch the yellow-slickered lobstermen standing in their boats to haul in their traps, rebait them, and toss them back into the ocean. Sometimes I watch sailboats race across the horizon from Falmouth to Monhegan Island and back again and, at night, the clouds racing past the moon.

Recently a contest was held at the island store to see who could identify the greatest number of the island's outhouses pictured in a long row of snapshots tacked up on a wall. I was told that people generally agreed the view from the nubble outhouse is one of the best on the island—an opinion seconded in the grateful graffiti left by occasional winter visitors—*pace* Ethan Groate.

His contrary response reminds me of an incident that occurred on a visit I made years ago to the great eighth-century Buddhist temple of Borobudur on the island of Java. In ninety degrees of muggy heat, sweat streaming from my pores, I climbed the steep shadeless hill up to the temple, then on around the temple's lavishly carved walls, examining the thousands of narrative and decorative stone bas-reliefs as I spiraled slowly up toward the summit. Growing progressively abstract and spiritual as they approached the top, the sculptures were so transporting that even the most obdurate materialist must feel the holiness of such a place. Back at the bottom, where a protective park with refreshment stands, parking lots, and rest rooms surrounded the temple, I stopped at a kiosk to gulp down a tall glass of hot lemon, and another, and yet another, then walked to the toilets before leaving. Squatting inside a booth, I overheard an American woman, one of a new busload of tourists, tell her companion that she'd rather hold it in for another hour than use these awful toilets. I was surprised: the tourist facilities in the park were modern and impeccable, the toilets scrupulously cared for, like everything at that holy site where UNESCO had carried out a careful restoration, hoping to preserve the temple and its grounds for another thousand years. "None of the toilets flush, they don't even have seats," wailed the tourist to her companion. Now, it was true that the toilets had no mechanical levers to release a rush of water—often far in excess of what might be needed—like those the tourists were used to. But there was plenty of clean water: in each booth, beside the toilet, stood a deep tiled cistern with a faucet that could be turned on as needed and a long-handled ladle for transporting the water to the toilet in the exact quantity needed for flushing. And a pair of slightly raised footrests were positioned for comfortably squatting over the low toilet bowl. An efficient sanitary system—like my privy, unfairly scorned by Ethan Groate.

As I sit high in my outhouse on the smooth seat, watching the frog-suited couple dive from their boat for sea urchins destined for the lucrative Japanese market, I'm both sitting and squatting. Since my midwife friend Margaret convinced me of the natural virtues of squatting to expel an object from the lower body, I've placed a four-by-four on the floor as a footrest, so my knees are raised to the level of my waist, I can rest my elbows on them, chin in my hands, and push. In our first summer here, we always threw a ladleful of lye down to the ground below before leaving the outhouse, as someone had advised; but with so few odors or insects, I no longer bother. Why fill up the space any sooner than necessary? When I decide to plant a garden, it will be behind the outhouse, where the rich night soil trickles down and enormous blackberries are just now beginning to ripen. I pick two, press them against the roof of my mouth with my tongue to release the juices, and savor them slowly as I walk back up the path to the cabin.

When the kettle's boiling I place a dishpan in one half of the double sink, fill it with warm soapy water, and pile in the dirty dishes. In the other half I set another dishpan under the pump for rinsing. The capacious cistern that serves as rain barrel holds more water than I'm ever likely to need; I've never once run out. All the same, I try to use the minimum. The pleasure is as much aesthetic as practical. Sinking my hands in the warm suds and reliving the meal as I whoosh away the remains, I think of the years in New York when I washed dishes with the taps wide open and the water running down the drain, oblivious of the energy required to purify an urban water supply, and then of other years when I routinely piled dishes into an electric dishwasher, though the time required to scrape and rinse them, then load, start, run, and empty the machine, compounded by the excess water and energy, the detergent pollution, noise, wear on the dishes, the cost of purchase, operation, and repair, and the eventual problem of solid waste disposal washed away the advantage, unless I had been feeding a mob.

Yet, if it hadn't cost half a fortune to get a rig up on the nubble for digging a well or to bury electrical and phone lines under the beach, Jerry would probably have installed all the standard equipment for an up-to-date life under late-twentieth-century capitalism, and I would never have discovered how gracefully one can live without them.

I empty the dishwater down the drain and wipe the sink, focusing not on the hairline cracks but on the islands of porcelain gleaming white between them. Let the Tax Appraiser file his report. This cabin, however scarred or outmoded, miraculously renews itself. Like my rib, which will soon be healed.

It's October 18—later than I've ever been on the island. Dense foggy mornings, frosty nights, a lucent crown of brilliant red and golden leaves on the distant ridge. A stately great blue heron arrives at dusk to fish the cove; hundreds of ducks mass offshore in a huge black armada; two cedar waxwings with their masked faces and jaunty crests swing on the ripened goldenrod burning across the nubble in the cool October light; honking geese V southward overhead—all preparing for winter. Soon, I fear, I too, succumbing to the cold, will have to pack and leave.

A storm rages that night, bringing heavy winds and

choppy seas. When it clears, the normally white beach is littered with masses of dark seaweed thrown up from the deep and other interesting debris that cause bathers to think post-storm beaches "dirty." (One summer, in fact, the city of Portland hired teams of teenagers to rake up and burn all the seaweed, driftwood, and refuse that had accumulated on South Beach during the previous winter, only to see much of it replaced during the next big storm. The one lasting result I could see of all that fruitless effort was the pitiful waste of the driftwood fuel I'd come to count on.) According to a booklet on seaweeds Jerry has kindly mailed up to me, many species of seaweed are exposed only after a storm; so at the next low tide I go down to the beach in my poncho to investigate.

The shore is strewn with balls of Irish moss, immense blades of smooth long-stemmed kelp, similar to the Japanese kombu, and several long whips of the rare sea plant I'd longed to find, alaria. This brown seaweed, sometimes called honey kelp, winged kelp, or, in Japanese, wakame, looks very like ordinary long-stemmed kelp but for the delicious hollow rib which is actually a continuation of the stem, or stipe, running from the holdfast all along the blade to the very tip and which, when sliced into a salad or stew, adds a sweet tasty crunch, something like water chestnuts.

When I've gathered all the alaria I can find, I crisscross the beach several times more looking for tangle and dulse, but without success, and pass up two more left-handed fisherman's gloves at their historic spot. Heading up the beach toward the nubble, I notice what looks like a giant quahog, the largest I've ever seen, lying alone like a rock in the midst of a great expanse of white sand at the top of the beach, far from the water.

I stoop to examine it. Its shell is open about half an inch, revealing the firm plump flesh of a living clam. I pick it up. Measuring eight or nine inches across, it lies in my hand like a stone weighing several pounds—equivalent in size to perhaps a dozen of my ordinary, laboriously procured clams. As soon as I poke the flesh the quahog snaps closed its shells, clamming up tight. I drop it into the bucket.

For years I've seen only ashtrays in those largest of all empty clam shells strewn along the shore, have passed them in ignorance, like most beachcombers, oblivious of their species or how they got there. I suppose I assumed they'd been snatched from the ocean by gulls and dropped from the sky—even though their smooth shells offer no purchase for a beak and seem far too heavy for a gull to lift. Now, remembering that storms can toss entire armadas onto shore, I wonder if perhaps the ocean itself hasn't somehow hurled it here.

Can it be safe to eat? With plants the trick is to avoid harmful species; but with shellfish it's the tainted individual one must guard against by making sure each specimen is alive and healthy when caught. This is not always as easy as it appears; it takes some practice to discover each species' telltale vital motions. Most creatures naturally retreat or flee when they sense danger: clams clam up, periwinkles slam shut their opercula, crabs scram; but (as humans have sometimes observed closer to home) some live creatures act dead and some dead ones look alive. Crustaceans that have just shed their shell go limp and simulate corpses, while lifeless empty bivalve shells are sometimes misleadingly glued shut by a cement of water and sand. To guard against these traps, I've learned to cook my bivalves separately; then, if an individual fails to open, or if a sand-filled one finds its way into the pot, I can remove the duds, let the sand sink, and skim off the good broth. Ordinarily I wouldn't consider eating a creature lacking any means of surface locomotion found so far from its underwater habitat; but this particular clam is so clearly alive and so loaded with meat—big enough for an entire meal—that I decide to risk it.

That evening I turn my catch into the sweetest chowder I've ever had. In the pot, it gives up a rich aromatic broth and yields over a cupful of nutty meat. I thicken the strained broth with gelatinous Irish moss (the same agent used commercially to thicken ice cream), add the chopped meat, flavor it with sea rocket, garlic, and angelica, and garnish it with six inches of crisp stipe of fresh alaria that I sliver with a paring knife. To the accompaniment of foghorns and buoy bells, beside a crackling fire, I slowly eat my dinner.

The next day I'm down at the shore hunting again. I find three more specimens of the giant clam, and the following day, two. I scrub them, steam them open, and anatomize them, examining each intricate organ before I eat them. I'm so absorbed that not till the third day do I turn to my books to see what I can find out about this newest and easiest catch. Gibbons, in an entire brief chapter devoted to its praises, tells me I have found not a quahog but a surf clam, the largest clam species on the Atlantic seaboard. Like so many wild foods, the surf clam is widely scorned by all but a few initiates—including Gibbons, and now myself. I'm pleased to find I've been chopping into my chowders parts of the clam that even Gibbons disdains as tough. From him I learn to sauté and savor unadorned the large tender cylindrical abductor muscles, the very part of the scallop we consume and prized by Gibbons in the surf clam as sweeter than the sweetest scallop's.

Tomorrow, according to the forecast, begins another week of cold with intermittent rain. Having already felt the first premonitory chill of winter, I'm resigned to boarding up and leaving for the city in at most a week. In the few remaining days I concentrate exclusively on surf clams, snatching them from cresting waves before the undertow can rush them out again. As I toss the empty shells out to sea, I wonder if and where they'll wash ashore to be collected for ashtrays by day-trippers ignorant of what they've found—like me until just this week. It troubles me that though I read Gibbons's book straight through, I never before noticed a surf clam. What other edible species may be lying unrecognized at my feet?

On Friday the sea turns calm, and there are no more clams.

BUNDLED up on the deck in parka, muffler, and gloves to capture the few precious hours of remaining light, I seem to have entered a new mode. I glance up from my book to notice the apple tree heavy with ripe fruit. But instead of being small and green, the apples are yellow, some tinted with delicate pale-pink stripes, some as large as market fruit. My surprise registers more as a feeling than as a thought. I reproach myself for having made no more than half a dozen apple pies this year, as many batches of applesauce, two apple cakes, only three jars of apple chutney, a few experimental savory dishes—and all mainly from windfalls, since I couldn't bear to pluck a fruit before its prime. And now the most perfect apples will go uneaten. (If I had a family to feed we could store our apples for the winter in bins, or dried, or preserved in chutneys, jams, and sauces. But alone I'm able to eat just so many apples.)

Seeing this vast casual waste, I feel a pang of regret—fleeting and dismissible, since I've had all the fruit I want. I let it go and return to my book. But glancing up to reflect on a passage, I see again the groaning tree and the pang returns, this time closer to a thought. Each time I look up it nags at me, expanding bit by bit into the space between my other thoughts, until finally I put down my book and try to grasp it. I focus on the feeling as I fill in one small gap after another, connecting what have hitherto been disparate, even contrary, takes, until at last it's there before me, full-blown as the apple tree itself: a long thought that lengthens and spreads like the sun's rays at day's end till it tints the entire sky—surely the kind of thought Ouspensky means by "long":

This island, which has been my refuge from the waste that is the other side of glut, produces excess of its own. There are all those apples, finally ripened to perfection, and they will not be eaten. Everywhere I look I see a world of astonishing abundance, wild extravagance, glorious waste. Hundreds of thousands of dock seeds, my muffin enricher, fringe the bluff. Touch-me-nots (or jewelweed) fling their edible seeds into the air at the merest touch of a bird or breeze. Brilliant red rose hips, my staple tea, my daily hit of Vitamin C, now entirely surround the cabin. They're already perfectly preserved, and though birds will feed on them all winter there'll still be plenty for me when I return in spring. Countless seaweeds, naturally dried and salted, line the shore; blackberry leaves, goldenrod, bay all beckon me to harvest and dry them for winter infusions. Everywhere I turn I see abundance and overflow—as excessive as the glut I deplore in the city, but with the crucial difference that here it's all biodegradable. Whatever I leave behind far from being wasted will nourish the soil and grow again.

From a few isolated tentative flashes, my thought has lengthened into an awareness of abundance that replaces the pang of regret with a purr of joy. And still, as long as I concentrate, it has plenty of room to grow—and will continue to grow and stretch until, after many more meals and years, it will eventually encompass a great cornucopia of edibles in perfect ecological balance spiraling in circles downward to the sea within a ten-minute radius of my hearth. Before I'm done I will have found and eaten: elderberries, raspberries, blackberries, huckleberries, currants, shadberries, rose hips, jewelweed, fiddleheads, goldenrod, sheep sorrel, charlock, bay leaves, all from the brush surrounding the cabin; then just down the stairs above the beach: angelica (for parsley), Scotch lovage, dandelion, chicory, beach peas, red clover, orach, lamb's-quarters, strawberry goosefoot, goosetongue, sea rocket, strand wheat, yellow dock, apples; in the tidal flats and among the rocks: steamer clams, quahogs, surf clams, green crabs, blue mussels, horse mussels, periwinkles, dog whelks, moon shells, sea urchins, lobsters, eels; in the tidal pools that form my seaweed garden: sea lettuce, tiger moss, Irish moss, tangle, bullwhip kelp, long-stemmed kelp; and strewn across the beach after a storm: alaria, purple dulse, laver or nori, and colonies of arame; then venturing across the beach, up the path, onto the dirt road: a dozen other varieties of apples, as well as pears, cattails, pineapple weed, juniper berries, serviceberries, cranberries, chokecherries, strawberries, staghorn sumac, Jerusalem artichokes, acorns, chestnuts; and in the woods: wild ginger, blueberries, mint, ground nut, wood sorrel, and various edible fungi. All are part of the living cohort I first glimpsed on the subway in its human manifestation and now see daily in myriad forms everywhere I look.

Not only on the nubble but everywhere, once I've learned how to see. In the cracks of city sidewalks, on the Colorado Rocky mountainsides, in the lawns of Cleveland Heights and the yards of Santa Fe, in the gutters of Honolulu, on the trails of Oahu, sprinkling the desert and lining the riverbanks, I see endless offerings of discarded or unharvested food: pigweed, nasturtiums, laurel, mint, watercress, prickly pears, plums, apricots, avocados, guavas, cherries, crab apples, oranges, lemons, pomegranates—a garden of delectables unrecognized, snubbed, forgotten by a world that goes to the store.

I decide to fill a garbage bag with a selection of dried seaweeds and a few small bags with dock seeds, rose hips, and bay leaves to take back to the city as a reminder of the difference between abundance and glut, between a long thought and a short one.

Now the wild spinach has all gone to seed and the nights have turned so cold that I fear the water will freeze and crack the cistern. I drain it, pack my bags, close off the propane, and before dusk falls reluctantly board up the cabin.

As I look back at the nubble from the end of the road where I wait for Lucy Chaplain to pick me up in the island taxi to take me and my gear to the ferry, I see the great blue heron light again at the base of the Shmoos. I unpack the binoculars to watch him fish. How majestically he stands on one foot in the roiling surf as the tide flows in. He wades through the water so slowly that his movement is almost imperceptible, though once I see him swat at something in the air with his great wing, then snatch it with his beak. Mostly he just waits and watches, patient and still, until the moment comes to plunge his head into the water to grab his prey and then, throwing back his head, consume it in a few snaps of his long beak. I watch his darkening silhouette with its stilt legs and slender throat until there's barely light to see by.

I want my thoughts to be as patient and slow as the heron standing at the water's edge fishing the incoming tide for as long as it takes to catch the treasures swimming by. Or I want them, like the barnacles opening up to feed when the tide comes in, to filter the plankton newly streaming around me, so rich and abundant that what I can't find here hardly seems worth wanting.

PART TWO

The Mainland

FIVE

So well had I adapted to the exacting circumstances of my summer life on the nubble that I thought it impossible to forget. But once I was back in the city, my confidence teetered.

The appearance of things had subtly changed. Park benches had been painted green. Long-familiar shops had changed hands. Skirts were long, hair sleek, and last year's colors had been replaced by colors popular a dozen years ago. I was shocked to find that the local public library, housed in a glorious Victorian building where my children had learned to love books, had drastically reduced its hours, and another neighborhood branch had closed altogether. Yet new buildings were rising toward the sky all over town; steam shovels and giant cranes worked double-time. And a new kind of restaurant had sprung up with expensive menus and a young, confident clientele. Sidewalks were more crowded, there were more street people, traffic felt more chaotic than when I had left. Voices, music, sirens, horns were louder, brasher, more frantic.

Afraid of losing my new tranquillity, I lined up on the spice shelf in my kitchen jars of rose hips, dock seeds, and bay leaves to remind me of how little I'd needed, and I placed in a prominent cupboard the bag of assorted seaweeds

I had so painstakingly collected and dried, intending to duplicate the soups and breads that had inspired and sustained me all summer. But with a deli on every other block purveying all sorts of ethnic breads, I never baked a single loaf. Had I been foolish, perhaps arrogant, to think it worthwhile to lug those dried vegetables back to New York? One look at the paltry health-food stores in Manhattan, compared to the extravagant consumer dens like Balducci's and Zabar's, with their huge selections of out-of-season fruits, exotic vegetables, luxury imports of meats, fish, game, cheeses, oils, condiments, and sweets from all over the world, and I saw what I was bucking. If I wasn't careful I'd slide back to my pre-nubble self—abandon solitary meditation, fit friends into time slots, stay up till all hours, clutter my head with movies, fill up the calendar, squander attention, water, food, paper, energy, time—no matter how much seaweed or dock I had stashed in the kitchen.

First my thumbnail went. I nibbled at its rough edges, trimming it down until, not two weeks back in the city, I had bitten it to the quick. One by one the other nails followed—taking with them my confidence to eschew everything but what I loved. What was it I loved? Steeped again in current events and the heavy weight of the world, I felt my memory grow fuzzy. All that time-consuming baking and cooking seemed pointless here, like solitude itself.

And no wonder. Except in my familiar dream of rooms, until that summer I'd never been alone and, in fact, had counted my best years those spent at the center of a densely crowded political movement.

I was in my thirties when I joined the political fray, several years after my world had shrunk down to the approximate size of a kitchen, a husband, and a nursery. Then it began to expand again, opening up to reveal room after room crowded with co-conspirators: the civil-rights movement, the anti-war movement, the women's liberation movement.

At first more an inquiry than a credo, the women's movement quickly grew into a loose community of stalwarts committed to act on certain basic understandings. Inside its shelter we were free to be not "women," despised and discounted, but ourselves. It felt like a miracle: one day we were all smeared with the female taint and its attendant humiliations, and the next we were out in the streets shouting No!—marching down Fifth Avenue, telling the world about our orgasms and abortions, tossing out our brooms and girdles, bringing suits to overturn laws, masterminding a takeover of *The Ladies' Home Journal*. Women? We gave them *women*! We organized secretaries, prostitutes, housewives, flight attendants. We integrated exclusive all-male establishments, taking on taverns, clubs, schools, entire professions. We challenged every newspaper, museum, and institution that denigrated or ignored us. The more serious our purpose, the more fun we had, pinching brokers and messengers at our lunchtime Whistle-In on Wall Street, forming all-woman bands, crowning a live sheep Miss America. As we radiated our strength to others through our simple, powerful ideas, I came to accept, embrace, even love this body and soul that were born with me, building a clean, powerful ego.

Then gradually, perhaps inevitably, with the passing years the vitality of the women's movement was sapped as our victories were taken for granted, our ideas co-opted or subverted, our quarrels magnified, our truths accepted as truisms and overlooked. We were walloped and then dragged by the heavy swing of the pendulum. That oppressive female taint, that sign like a yellow star I had felt as a girl hooked on appearances, and again as a political activist representing a "special interest," and as a writer of "women's books," soon appeared once again on whatever women do. Not two weeks back in New York I heard a big burly war veteran, representing the War Resisters League on a panel discussing War and Peace, lower his voice to confess to an overflowing room that perhaps the best thing women can do for peace is get the hell out of the peace movement, or at least lie low, because as long as the peace movement belongs to women, men will flee it and instead make war and rule the world.

So the movement born to obliterate the taint itself became tainted:

Hey, whatever happened to the women's liberation movement?

The what?

You know. The women's movement. Why aren't people interested anymore?

Oh, that. You see, what happened is, it became tainted.

By what?

By its close association with women.

What a relief it had been, then, to be alone at the nubble, where there was hardly anyone to take the part for the whole. What a relief to have that weight of womanhood rise like a gull and fly away. To be where nothing I did had a scripted meaning. Where keeping house and cooking were not female chores but simple tasks of pleasure and survival. Where the books I read were not highbrow, lowbrow, tough or soft, but simply books. Where my clothes were not for dress-up or lounging, for night or day (often when the temperatures dropped I would wear my daytime sweater through the night), not masculine or feminine, youthful or dowdy, but merely clothes. In my solitude, the freedom that had been the movement's promise was extended and topped: after the freedom that comes from strengthening ego came the freedom that comes from dropping it.

No wonder that even after the winter chased me back to New York a phantom part of me clung to the island, pursuing serendipitous shellfish and serpentine thoughts. Though I was alone in my apartment, with the children off at college and Jerry working in Texas, it wasn't the same solitude. I did relish the long steamy soak I took the hour I arrived home in New York, the crisp bedsheets, the bright steady light available at the mere flick of a switch, and the exciting (if sometimes disturbing) street scenes; but I was afraid to become a traitor to my newest self. Either a traitor or a teller of tales about winkles and weeds that no urbanite I knew could understand—not even my closest feminist friends. To those tough-minded fast-talking Manhattanites the language of the nubble would probably sound "mushy," as talk of love sounds to little boys. Their rapid-fire thoughts were sometimes brilliant as comets, but I was trying to slow mine down to a halt; instead of honing distinctions, I was learning to see beyond them. The very words I needed to describe my experience—words like *simple, whole, spiritual*—were sure to embarrass my friends or alarm them, as my letters had alarmed Katherine.

Brooding at the window, I recalled a night decades earlier when I returned home after midnight from my first thrilling meeting at the beginning of the women's liberation movement to face Jerry's suspicious questions. Back home in my comfortable apartment, where for years I had tried to be a compliant and dutiful wife, I sensed that if I were to explain to my husband what had really gone on in the Lower East Side tenement I had just come from, if I were to tell him how excited I was by the ideas that had filled the room, he would feel threatened, take it as an open challenge to his authority, a betrayal tantamount to a declaration of war. I was not prepared for war. It was too soon; the children were too young; I was afraid. So instead I turned temporary traitor to my liberators, and staring out this very window to avoid Jerry's eyes, I ridiculed the brave, outrageous ideas I had raptly listened to that night, hoping to disguise how deeply they had already affected me.

Now again I feel torn in two. How can I hold on to my newfound freedom? How brace myself against the seductive distractions and dangers of New York—the stimulating conversations, rugged politics, gutsy confrontations; the music, art, noise, speed, and all the discordant energies of a beguiling and diverse humanity?

When the phone rings I leap—then hesitate, trying to resist. It's Katherine, calling to announce our next women's group meeting. I scribble down the date, even though I suspect that the price of preserving my new life may be dropping out of the old. Beginning with the dearest part, my women's group.

AMY comes home for the weekend, and my conflict abates; I never doubt who I am when my children need me. I fix us a dinner I know she'll like: spicy chicken, yellow rice, arugula salad, pecan pie. Not having seen my daughter since May, I want to hear everything. Over dinner she tells me about her new roommates, her classes and teachers, and finally about her agony over having to decide on a major by December. I listen, replacing my concerns with hers as I take in her every word, gesture, toss of the head. Can this tall long-haired beauty be the same person I suckled and taught to read? How, she frets, can she possibly choose a major by December when she can't decide what she wants to do with her life.

"It doesn't matter what you choose," I advise. "You can always change your mind later."

"No I can't. After December it will be too late to switch."

"Don't be silly, it's never too late. You can go on switching all your life. Look at me. I've just made one of the biggest changes of all—and at fifty!" Wanting her to know how much more flexible time may be than she thinks it is, I spread out on the table my seaweed, rose hips, and dock seeds in an effort to convey the flavor and flair of my new life.

"Mom!" she breaks in fiercely. "How can you get so carried away? Next year it'll be something else," she accuses, finding me not flexible but flighty.

For safety's sake, children want their parents predictable (as parents want their children), while for myself I want the opposite. Indeed, sometimes I view my life as a set of unpredictable leaps—beginning at twenty, when to escape a likely suburban marriage I fled Ohio to join the free spirits in New York's Greenwich Village. Again, at thirty, when just in time, as I was slipping into the pit of dependence with an infant on each hand, I pulled myself up by the combat bootstraps of activism. Then in my fortieth year, when the world's indulgent smile to youth deserted me, threatening to leave me forever "just a housewife" (a status no number of freelance jobs or unpublished stories could mitigate), in that very year I published my first novel. Now each book I write takes me deep into new territory. But does this mean I'm flighty? Or is Amy's exasperation really over something else—perhaps my extended absence?

The next day, Saturday, we go shopping. Amy needs shoes, boots, a winter coat. We go to Eighth Street—

former site of many unusual bookstores and handmade-sandal shops, now home to a book-chain bookstore and eighteen shoe shops, also mostly chains. After successfully scouring the stores for two pairs of handsome shoes, we are resting before a cleverly got-up window full of outrageous jewelry, a hangover of the old bohemian Eighth Street of my youth. "Now I want to give *you* a present, Mom," says Amy. "There's a pair of earrings I want to buy you—but first you'll have to get your ears pierced."

"Me? Have my ears pierced? Are you crazy? After getting through my whole life with clip-ons?"

"Mom!" she says, pulling her brows together like her father. "You're always telling me it's never too late. Now it's about time you got your ears pierced. You are fifty years old! This will be my birthday present to you."

She begins to tug at my arm. I laugh and resist, but not too strenuously. "What about buying your coat?"

"Afterward," she says. When she's got me headed in the right direction she opens a door, holds it with her foot, and edges me into a narrow shop. And before I know it I'm sitting stiffly in a chair while a slim man with rows of earrings in both his ears prepares to shoot gold studs into my earlobes with what looks like a staple gun.

"Will it hurt?"

"A pinprick."

I brace myself as he shoots. Surprisingly, it doesn't hurt. In fact, I feel giddy: grateful for my daughter's gift. When she tells me that I have now changed forever my Euler number (the number of holes in a mathematical object) by adding these two new orifices to my body, I'm so glad to be updated that I wonder if I shouldn't have more holes punched on every birthday, maybe one in my nose as well.

• • •

SYLVIA buzzes me into the lobby of her SoHo loft building. A bit late, I hope they haven't started. We're usually prompt, pretty disciplined. A combination study and political-action group composed mostly of veterans of the movement's early days, we formed seven years ago with the ambitious goal of revitalizing the flagging feminist movement itself. I enter the elevator and press 3. I'm apprehensive. This feels like a family affair. Sometimes lately we even call ourselves a family because, given the deterioration of the political climate, we're hardly a vanguard anymore. As in a family, complaint and affection have replaced our inquiring edge.

I think of my original family, whom I left in Cleveland decades before, placing my childhood values on hold. Although the new values I embraced in the women's movement seemed at first to estrange me further from the old, eventually, as I learned more and more about myself and families, I reconciled the two. Now, pressing the buzzer of 3C, I wonder if I'm attempting a repeat performance: cutting loose from my political "family" in order to expand again.

Sylvia opens the door and lets out a squeal of welcome. "You're back! You're so brown! Your hair's grown! Tell us everything."

I embrace her and then the others, feeling like a guilty lover whose heart has changed. Since my writing life developed in the movement, my resolve to be alone might seem like ingratitude, defection, perhaps that very political retreat we came together to oppose. After meeting weekly for years to promote resistance to life as it is, how will these women view my embracing acceptance and making do—like George Sand, a flaming feminist of another time, whose goal was "acceptance of life, whatever it be"?

Our custom at the first meeting after summer break is to go around the room catching up on one another's lives before discussing projects for the coming year. I listen as each one pours out her news. When my turn comes I take a deep breath and plunge in. They're excited for me as I describe the new world I uncovered between the tides. I can feel them with me as I tell my joy in living alone on mussels and weeds. But when I try to describe how time slowed to a standstill, replacing the mess of history with something timeless, ageless, eternal, I begin to see baffled expressions. Extolling the ecstatic feelings I discovered in solitude, as mind-expanding as those we all experienced together in the early days of the movement, explaining how my anxieties and conflicts melted away in my recognition that I'm part of one vast interconnected whole, I see Sylvia, Barbara, Carey, even Katherine exchanging looks.

I heave a sigh of resignation, knowing how notoriously difficult it is to put unity into words. I've known it since my first vision on the subway. The language needed to describe unity is itself divisive, each word an island proclaiming its difference from every other. Words tumble out singly, one after another; compared to the infinity of stillness they are crude, noisy things—which is why the name of God cannot be spoken, why "the tao that can be told is not the eternal Tao," why silence is the truest mystic state. Seeing my friends' puzzled concern, I imagine I must sound to them like a member of some West Coast cult or utopian religious sect. The more I try to explain, the more I feel the language gap widen, leaving me isolated and estranged.

Finally, invoking my fifty years, a number shockingly old to most of them, I announce that henceforth I intend to do only what I love regardless of what anyone thinks. Unfortunately, I explain, lack of insulation and water in my Maine cabin has forced me back to the city for the winter, but my hope is somehow to preserve here the sense of life I attained on the island. And because it's so difficult for me to hold on to this in face of New York's seductive attractions (beginning, I tell them, with you), I'm taking an indefinite leave of absence from our group—starting immediately.

I rush out as soon as the meeting's over and, through a haze of toxic fumes, trudge uptown to the charged dissonant songs of taxi horns and sirens, past throngs of shoppers eyeing neon windows, toward a fluorescent blaze of skyscrapers. White light edges the gay scallops of the Chrysler tower, orange and green lights decorate the Empire State's, white, yellow, red, and green lights flash and sparkle up the avenues, obliterating every star. Am I more exhilarated or depressed by such spectacular waste of energy? Paper trash whips against my ankles as gusty winds speed me across SoHo into the side streets of the West Village where shivering homeless search methodically through overflowing trash baskets, without benefit of St. Joseph the Provider. Inside my apartment, I hang up my coat and, hoping to recycle a salvaged Tuesday night, go straight to the computer.

My friend Katherine calls me for lunch. An editor on a women's magazine, she says she has a project in mind for me. Hearing the concern in her voice, I wonder if her true project isn't to induce me back to the group.

We meet at a crowded sushi restaurant near her office. Sushi, I observe, is just what I eat on the island in a different form: rice, shellfish, seaweed.

"Seaweed?" asks Katherine.

"Sure. The nori they wrap around sushi is seaweed."

"Oh, so it is," she says skeptically, looking down her chopsticks. Artful makeup deepens her dark eyes and accents her naturally protuberant cheekbones; her clothes, jewelry, scarves, shoes point toward the future. Without mentioning my leave from the group, she asks me how I'd like to write an essay about wild cuisine for a special food issue of the magazine. "I could send a photographer out, maybe do a big spread: Independent Woman Lives by Her Wits, or something."

A photographer on the nubble? Before I can refuse, Katherine urges me to take my time thinking it over. "I'm going away for a week and can't do anything anyway till I get back."

"Where are you going?"

"To Kansas City to see my mom. We're quite worried about her, actually."

I lean forward to hear her story. For years, Katherine confides, Katherine's mother has been a problem to her children, ever since her husband left her for a younger woman. Now she's suddenly gotten worse, more and more reclusive. Lately she stays in her house for days on end, goes out only to get food. When people drop by to see her, she sends them away. If they come back, she goes upstairs and won't answer the door.

"What's the matter with that?" I ask.

Katherine glares at me. "It's sick," she says, folding her arms.

I back down. "What does she do by herself?"

"Nothing. That's the problem."

"Nothing?"

"Well, you know, she watches TV, reads, does the crosswords, bakes. She's getting fat, too. No exercise. We've got to decide what to do about her."

"Maybe she's happier by herself. Maybe this is what she always wanted to do but never had the chance."

"That's insane," Katherine bristles. "Being alone like that is not good for anyone, but especially not my mother. Her family was always everything to her. Now she won't see her own sons or even her grandchildren unless they make a date in advance. She refuses to cook for them, too. This year she told them she wants *them* to do Christmas."

When I laugh, Katherine says, "I think she should get some therapy. I'm going to try to convince her to see someone."

"But Katherine," I protest, "maybe she prefers her own company. Or maybe she's tired of being the mama after all these years. Anyway, what's the matter with being reclusive? What's wrong with it?"

Katherine sets her jaw and stares at me. "It's just wrong," she says, weighting each word. Anxiety lines her brow. "Something is terribly wrong."

IT'S at a crowded Upper West Side Christmas party of a childhood friend, a two-turkey affair, that I finally come to terms with the seaweed mocking me from my cupboard.

I've just filled my plate for a second time with rich holiday fare when I see across the living room a woman who was my playmate back in Ohio during the first seven years of our lives. Even though the last time we saw each other was by chance twenty-five years ago on a subway, and before that when we were children, I immediately recognize Ella's striking face: olive skin, shapely, slightly parted lips, darting eyes set rather close together, high-bridged blade of a nose, long dark hair straight and shiny as a Navaho's.

As soon as she spots me coming toward her, her face too lights up with recognition. She beams as we carry our plates off to a corner to fill each other in on our lives, which, it turns out, have followed similar trajectories. She too is a writer: a play of hers is about to be produced Off-Broadway; she too has two children (daughters), one in college, one still in high school; like us, she and her husband have lived mostly apart for a number of years and now that the children are almost grown are considering divorce. Most surprising of all, she has become a Buddhist.

A Buddhist! I've never known a Buddhist or any sort of mystic in New York, only cynics, skeptics, Christians and Jews, mostly lapsed. Eagerly I pull Ella over to an empty couch to hear her story, then try to summarize for her the surprising changes I've just undergone. She listens attentively, nodding with what I take for understanding as I describe how, just when I thought the world was closing me out, a whole new world, quite as entrancing as the previous one, opened up to me. "I felt myself come alive again on the island. I began to see how everything is connected, how everything I need is right there—all that food and pleasure—free for the asking. But here—I don't know—I'm divided. It's slipping away from me, no matter how hard I try to hold on." Then I tell her about the rose hips and seaweed in my New York kitchen that I never remember to use, don't seem to care about anymore. "I'm afraid I'm losing it. And I can't talk about it to anyone, either; no one here understands." I feel my voice catch. "I don't know what to do. If only I'd been able to stay up there by myself."

"Tell me," says Ella, laying a hand on my arm. "Don't you like New York?"

"Like it! Until this year I thought it was the only place I could ever stand to be. You know—'a day away is a day lost'? But now . . . I don't know. There are so many distractions. There's no time to think. It's so hard to write here with all the stimulation, people to see, things to do. I've cut way back, but still every thought gets interrupted. And the island seems so remote. Less than two months back and I can't even remember the names of my wild foods. And all that good seaweed I collected just sits in a bag in the cupboard, taking up space. How I wish—"

My friend puts down her fork and looks me in the eye. I envy her calm composure—something I haven't felt since I left the island. "But that's attachment, don't you see? You've forgotten what you learned. You're clinging to your island, trying to keep it with you. It can't be done. Since you're here now, you should enjoy New York. Don't fight it. Everything you need is right here, too. And when you go back to your island, enjoy what's there. Forget about seaweed, it's just a stand-in for what you felt last summer."

I stare at her while she spreads two crackers with pâté.

"And as long as you're here," she says, smiling, as she offers a cracker to me, "you could begin by sampling Judy's absolutely sensational duck pâté."

How futile to have thought to preserve my new life by eating a bagful of seaweed, as if it were the body or blood of the nubble. Clinging to the island is like clinging to youth—no wonder I sometimes feel depressed. Yet try as I may to infuse my city life with its former excitement, rewarding a successful day at the computer with thick espresso at my favorite neighborhood café or a trip to the farmers' market for Belgian endive or Italian arugula, I can't quite pull it off. Time returns with its loud tick, and though I haunt the bookstores as I used to do and fill my evenings with music and news, at night I keep dreaming my dream of rooms.

Then even my dream is interrupted. It's an early morning in February; the ringing phone jolts me awake. "I hope I'm not waking you, hon," says Jerry, and I know from his voice it's trouble even before he blurts out his news: the company he works for is closing its Texas operation and moving him back to New York. Fortunately, they're planning to keep him on as a freelance; unfortunately, he too will be working at home.

What are we to do? One apartment and two claims to it. Our arrangements are thrown into complete turmoil. Jerry's job, which for years has returned him to New York infrequently enough to keep us friends yet frequently enough to keep us married, is now threatening the balance. How can our marriage, affectionate but exhausted, survive the strain of such proximity? Even with the best of wills we're bound to crowd each other—especially since the children, our major bond, no longer live at home.

Is this the moment to divorce? Though this is the very stuff of the novel I'm working on, I tremble. Which is more destructive of tranquillity—the raging agitations of divorce or the submerged ones of enforced cohabitation after years of freedom?

Calling on our reserves of affection and sympathy, once Jerry is back in New York we search for a solution by which we can remain as we've been: together apart, or apart together. Round and round we go (sitting at the window of what for years has been my office but Jerry now ominously reverts to calling "the study") until finally we agree to look for two adjacent places—or even one loft large enough to divide into two separate units—to replace the single large apartment we no longer need now that the children are grown.

But oh! Manhattan real estate! We pore over the Sunday *Times* week after week, we turn ourselves over to agents, we search all of downtown Manhattan, but we can find nothing both suitable and affordable, no two small places for the price of one large. And so, at the end of that difficult winter, when Jerry proposes to divide our apartment in two, I agree.

On paper it seems a perfect solution—civilized, reasonable, daring. We have avoided divorce for a decade by a deft combination of lucky circumstance and creative thinking; perhaps we can do it again. There's no telling how long we can keep this marriage alive—on condition that we live apart. After my season on the island I think I know what I truly need in order to live: not space, not charm, not even the usual trappings of convenience; what I need are peace and privacy—both now hostage to this incessant and unnerving search for real estate. If we don't have to move, I think, we may save a year of disruption and probably that much again of contention.

Plans go forward. We consult an architect, laying our current floor plan before her and describing our needs. In three weeks she has a blueprint—involving tearing down walls, putting up others, installing doors, closets, a second kitchen—and an enormous fee.

"But that's nonsense," I say, remembering how little I needed to live on only months before. Bending over the architect's drawing, I offer a counter plan. "We already have two bathrooms and two separate entrances. Now, if we just put a wall right there"—I point to a spot in the center—"then we can accomplish the same thing. One of us can have this side and the other that, and it probably won't cost more than a couple hundred dollars."

And it's true. Our pre-war apartment is spacious, with windows on three sides and a central hallway that roughly bisects the rooms. If we promise each other to keep the doors closed between the communicating rooms, at a wave of our magic wills we'll have two separate apartments in place of one. And when the children come home for vacation, we can simply fling open the doors and once again be a family.

We draw close together to complete our plans. By the time crocuses appear in the florist shops, and I start to think about leaving for the nubble, we're in such accord over the Wall that Jerry promises to have the alterations completed before I return again to the city in autumn.

SIX

How many years has it been since I tossed the baseball bat on the woodpile, dropped my fears, and came to terms with the hacker? So much time—more than a decade!—and as packed with events as any in my life. Years when my mother survived a hysterectomy and took up art, my father reluctantly retired at the age of ninety, Stevie injured his knees and became a scientist, my only brother died of cancer. And I, having freed myself from the grip of the city by thriving on the nubble, became an itinerant teacher—two years in Colorado, a month in Vermont, another in Arizona, a year in Hawaii, a semester in Ohio—while menopause quietly came and went. I wrote another book, saw AIDS rise and Communism fall, became a grandmother at sixty, and cheered as our movement woke from its long sleep to rally half a million marchers in Washington, D.C., in defense of reproductive rights, the nation's largest demonstration of any kind since the demonstrative Sixties.

Yet each spring when I return to the island, as soon as I pull my shopping cart over the tiny stream at the end of the dirt road and start across the sand, the years reduce to a moment as if I've never been away. No sooner have I pried the winter boards off the cabin doors, tied on my hat, and carried my bucket down to the beach than all the intervening time, no matter where I might have spent it or what shocking changes may await me on the island, fades and dissolves like a dream upon waking.

Back when marijuana was our diversion of choice, I often noticed, lighting up with a friend, that even after a long hiatus we could pick up our conversation and mood exactly where we'd left off the last time we'd smoked together. Every nuance and joke returned intact, reducing the time in between to background shading as we tuned in the special channel in the brain that could only be accessed by us and our drug. Once, sharing a joint in a San Francisco hotel room where I was stopping for some interviews, my old friend Terry and I gained total recall of the circumstances attending the previous joint we'd smoked together at a conference in Boston, eight years before—right down to the seating arrangements in the room, the clothes we wore, the meals we ate, and the words each of us said. Just so, despite my loss over the winter of even such essentials of nubble life as the names of the plants I live on, each time I return I tune right into the channel that plays back everything that ever happened to me here; time slows down, the names roll back in with the first taste, and the summers merge into one continuous present.

How then mark and remember the passage of time? I sometimes try to distinguish my nubble years according to their chief events: the year I found the mussels, the year South Beach turned to rock, the year of the searing heat, the year of the mosquitoes, the year of the brown-tail moth, the year Mars hung close to Earth like a red balloon. But as events began to repeat and merge in memory, to keep track of them and their order I had to construct a list, identifying events by the number of their year, as my father always did, amazing me as a child with what I took to be mysterious feats of memory back when I believed he knew everything: "The Crash happened in October 1929," he might say, or, "Grandpa arrived in Cleveland in 1896," or "Aunt Rose and Uncle Roy were married in the fall of '39." "But how do you know it was *that* year?" I would ask, bewildered. "Because," he'd shoot back without a blink, "we moved into our house in the spring of '37"—and I would try to fathom the secret of his astonishing ability to attach a number to each and every event. For myself, in those days when my life was still short, I was able to keep track of the annual revolutions by counting backward on my fingers through events alone: third grade, second grade, the summer I fell into the big pool, the Christmas Evan Claybert's wirehaired terrier got hit by a car, the birth of my cousin Dan, first grade, when I wet my pants in recess, kindergarten, the year we moved—not realizing that once I had lived through enough years it would become inefficient, if not impossible, to keep on counting back event by event without the aid of a numbering system. In due course, like everyone else I began to order my life by numbers: dating school papers, diary entries, and letters in the correct form, checking the clock, marking my calendar well in advance, dating my memories, until I too became so adept at the customary annual-chronological recording system that I could recall a place and aura simply by invoking a name (the Fifties, say, or May 1968, or New Year's Eve 1979), as prisoners are said to get laughs merely by shouting out numbers they've assigned to old jokes.

But when I'm alone on the island, even more than in my childhood, the numbers seem pointless. Why check my watch or calendar when I have nowhere to go and no one to meet? The names assigned to the days of the week, like the numbers assigned to the hours of the day, matter less to me than the height of the tides which peak, like the rising of the moon, a scant hour later every day. Since I wake to daylight, eat when I'm hungry, gather what's ripe, build a fire when I'm cold, and read what and when I like, the tides are a better clock, the sun and moon more useful calendars than the numbered ones.

Of course, there are always exceptions. Like the dated documents that mark the summer Jerry and I filed for divorce.

As I step off the ferry onto the island in my second spring alone, my first return, I feel like a lover coming home to my love. Retrieving my shopping cart from the cellar of the store, where it winters over, I stock up on some basic groceries, then wait in front of the store for the taxi.

"Hop in," shouts Lucy Chaplain, throwing open the door of her van. I load in the groceries, fold up the cart, and we're off.

Lucy clutches the wheel firmly as she zooms up the hill onto the dirt road and down again, straight across the island toward the sea. A small sinewy woman not much older than I, wearing harlequin glasses of another age, she has to stretch her neck to see over the hood of the speeding van, which gives her profile, with its thrust-out chin, a determined look. Through years of diligent work, in crises I can't even imagine, she has earned the respect of all the islanders, men and women alike: it is said she's never failed to meet a ferry, not even in hurricanes. Every day she lugs the mail in heavy canvas bags down to the dock and on and off the boats, delivers newspapers and freight, carries all messages. She has buried a husband, raised her children. Executing a snappy turn, she stops abruptly where the road dead-ends. She jumps out and begins depositing my gear and groceries on the road as I fumble to pay her. We shake hands; then with a fast wave she guns the motor and has already disappeared before I have even unfolded the shopping cart.

I load the cart practically to toppling and roll it across the stream into the arms of my beloved solitude.

Out on the rocks young herring gulls enact their mysterious spring ritual: almost squatting, they repeatedly raise their dark heads toward their mothers' white-feathered breasts as they loose thin juvenile wails. What does it mean? I think of my own children and the Wall. Though Jerry and I have managed to avert a collision by deftly dancing around our fears, electing to share instead of fight, there's no guarantee that the Wall will work. A Wall—particularly one that depends for its strength on the goodwill of two volatile people—can tumble down or, like a seesaw, tip off balance and crash to the ground if one person abandons the game.

When I'm halfway across South Beach suddenly everything turns wrong. Large dark rocks by the thousands stud the shore in place of the white sand that's always blanketed this beach. Where have they come from? How did they get here? Have they been rolled in by the ocean like surf clams, or have they been here all along hidden under surface sand that's inexplicably disappeared? Have the dunes that fringe the beach grown higher? Or do they only look different because they're naked, without a sign of vegetation? The plants that have made me feel one with the wild are nowhere in sight—gone like the sand, or are they still in their winter sleep, about to wake up like the apple tree, now sparkling with white blossoms, which I last saw dripping with fruit? Before I've even crossed the beach these questions have routed my winter agitations.

I open up the cabin, breathing in roses; as soon as I'm out of my traveling clothes I head back to the shore to inspect. None of the beach greens I planned to live on are where they belong, no orach or goosefoot or sea rocket. What will I do? But as I round a bend beyond the apple tree, I find the bank edging Skip Stone Beach dotted with the first young spikes of dandelion. I taste a leaf: not a trace of the bitterness I've grown to expect. But then, I've never before come early enough to find them so young. Excited, I wonder if I'm also in time for fiddleheads, edible only before they unfurl, or the wild asparagus I've never yet found, and other early-spring delicacies I've just read about on the ferry in my new field guide, *Wild Edible Plants of New England*.

As it's approaching dinnertime, I fill a pot with the slender jagged dandelion leaves that have graced European markets for centuries and wonder why they're despised by most Americans, who dig them out of their lawns by the roots and destroy them. Growing four feet tall by mid-July with a dozen or more flower buds to a stalk, these large hardy specimens (or are they the larger, closely related sow thistles?) will give me food from early spring till late autumn. First the earliest leaves in salads; then the sautéed crowns, those nascent centers of the developing stalk; then all summer long the newly emerging leaves which, though bitter, can be made palatable by cooking in several changes of water and mixing with sweet or zippy onion; and the jaunty flower buds. I have to keep picking the buds anyway to keep them from opening into flowers, which take up the nutrients, turning the leaves excessively bitter. Sautéed with garlic, these tangy morsels (my Skip Stone popcorn) make a crisp hors d'oeuvre, or, briefly boiled, an interesting addition to soups and stews. As long as I keep the buds from blossoming, this golden goose will produce new buds and leaves all the way through the autumn frosts—at which time, miraculously, the leaves lose their bitterness and can again be eaten raw, as in early spring, whether or not the plant has flowered. Even the roots, which at any time of year can be cooked like carrots, sautéed like potatoes, roasted and ground like coffee, or scrubbed and sliced into salads, are good. Though I'm reluctant to uproot anything I rely on —which may explain my staying married—dandelions are so hardy and plentiful here that I can certainly afford to dig myself some roots.

Farther down the cove hundreds of periwinkles move slowly over the black rocks, feeding on kelp. Unprotected and exposed, they're much easier and faster to harvest than mussels. With the tide coming up and the sun going down I stop right there and load my bucket.

Not that periwinkles and mussels are interchangeable—one is a snail and one a bivalve—no more than are shrimp with lobster, or potatoes with yams, or any species with any other—or, for that matter, any individual with any other. But periwinkles, with their affinity for garlic, make an equally delectable pasta sauce, and even though a periwinkle has a fraction of the meat found in a mussel, they can be scooped up like jacks, yielding a meal's worth in less time than it takes to locate a mussel bed.

On the other hand, the ease of harvesting periwinkles turns out to be more than matched by the time-consuming task of extracting the meat from their shells—as I'm now doing, seated on a boulder under a mottled sunset, nail in one hand, periwinkle in the other, tin cup between my knees. I've steamed them to the exact point where the operculum, the trapdoor that encloses the body in the shell, falls away, but not so long that the meat breaks up when I try to get it out. The delicate process of twisting each morsel out of its convoluted shell on the tip of a thin nail, jinxed by the slightest overcooking, wipes out whatever time I may have "saved" in harvesting them rather than mussels, which practically fall out of their shells when cooked—

another instance of the rule of balance I'm beginning to observe in this abundant corner of the universe: effort saved in one direction is spent in another.

As the corkscrew meats accumulate in the cup and the delicately colored shells pile up at my feet, examples multiply. If I pick sorrel by the speedy handful instead of slowly, leaf by leaf, then discarding blade by blade the unwanted grasses and roots in my hand wipes out the savings. A small crab has far less meat than a large one, but since small crabs usually have softer shells I can eat the small ones shells and all, eliminating the painstaking process of picking out the meat. (Besides, a woman in her fifties needs that extra calcium supplement that comes in shells.) The abundant new beach peas edging Skip Stone Cove are so tiny it would take forever to shell a cupful, but fortunately at that stage I can eat them like snow peas, pods and all; by the time the pods have grown too tough to eat, the mature peas inside are big enough to warrant shelling—though by then worms also find them worth the trouble. Or windfall apples, so easy to gather from the ground but sometimes rotting or wormy compared to the unblemished but far less accessible tree-borne fruit. There's always a reward to balance the cost, a trade-off among ease, size, quality, quantity—not to mention pleasure, that elusive factor whereby often what takes the most trouble and time yields the most satisfaction, like the breads that take hours to bake but permeate the cabin with their comforting aromas all day long, or cozy wood fires that must be continually tended, or the longest thoughts, or the sweetest love.

I laugh to see my efficient, urban self conducting time-motion studies of pleasure. And for the pleasure of it I apply my rule to the urban world of glut. Telephone-answering machines, intended to make phoning more efficient, double the number of phone calls made. Computers, expected to conserve paper (and eventually replace books), spit out whole forests of extra printouts. The so-called Green Revolution, by concentrating agricultural production and relying on chemicals, depletes the soil, pollutes the water, and diminishes the variety of available foods. Highways, developed to ease traffic, multiply traffic by enticing more drivers out on the roads. Airplanes, promoted to save travel time, increase it as people spend more time traveling than ever before. As Bertrand Russell observed of all transportation technology, each improvement only increases the distance you must go to get your daily business done. Sometimes speedy life whizzes you along so fast that nothing registers, like landscape from a speeding car or meaning in a speed-read text, so that every saving in time is paid for in lost experience. Perhaps time saved and time lost cancel each other out analogously to the biological rule described by Stephen Jay Gould:

> Small and large mammals are essentially similar. Their lifetimes are scaled to their life's pace, and all endure for approximately the same amount of biological time. Small mammals tick fast, burn rapidly, and live for a short time; large ones live long at a stately pace. Measured by their own internal clocks, mammals of different sizes tend to live for the same amount of time . . . each living at the appropriate pace of its own biological clock. . . . All mammals, regardless of their size, tend to breathe about 200 million times during their lives.

Examples of this universal balancing act keep proliferating, stretching out my meditation as I shell periwinkles. The invention of writing, Plato suggests, vastly reduced our individual powers of memory, and jet lag, which can reduce to a blur entire days, is the price we pay for excessive long-distance speed. My mind is humming and my mouth watering as I pick a sprig of newly leafed angelica to flavor the sauce and a blade of kelp to thicken it, then climb up to the kitchen to fete my return.

A big storm hits, and when it's over the sand is back on South Beach, except near the low-tide line where boulders and rocks still fringe the shore. At last the beach greens I count on for salads are coming up, more every day. The translucent yellow of the mustard flowers shimmers across the nubble. As the days lengthen, moving slowly toward the summer solstice, I feel my powers compounding, my tranquillity returning, until, when I take up my manuscript, connections stream into my mind and sometimes onto the page.

Then one morning as I'm doing my stretches I hear a dire warning on the radio. The red tide—a deadly organism fatal to humans, carried by tainted bivalves, including mussels and clams—has arrived on the coast. The announcer explains that by attacking the central nervous system it paralyzes the vital organs. All bivalves taken from Atlantic beaches and clam beds as far south as Virginia have been ruled off-limits until further notice.

What shall I do? I've been eating mussels every day for weeks; they're my staple, my manna, and mussel broth my basic stock. How can I give them up? Periwinkles too? Crabs? I look out over the water: it's as pristine and blue as the sky, without a hint of red; two lobster boats are chugging through Shark Cove, the lobstermen setting their traps exactly as they always do. All the same, I tentatively decide to forgo shellfish and inquire around.

At the store no one seems concerned. (But none of them eats mussels, either.) The storekeeper, feeling sorry for me, offers me some frozen deep-water shrimp from his private stash as a mussel substitute. "This should keep you alive another day, anyway," he says, winking.

When Richard Mann drives his army truck out to the nubble two days later to replace my empty propane tanks with full ones and check my lamps for leaks, I ask him about the red tide. A big skilled thoughtful man, a native islander, he reads the sea and sky as some of my New York friends read the *Times*.

Richard lays his wrench down on the table and laughs at my question. "It's a lot of hogwash if you ask me. For years they've been saying all of Casco Bay is off-limits. Supposedly you can be arrested and fined for taking any mussels or clams at all. But lots of folks around here eat them all the time, and I never heard of a one of them getting sick."

"Would you eat them yourself?"

"Don't much like them myself. But my kids do. Specially clams."

"And you'd give them to your kids? When the red tide's in?"

"Yup, anytime, long as they look okay. When I want clams I just go over to Judson Cove and dig me some." I follow him to another hanging lamp, and while he tightens the fittings he tells me about old Pood Bricker, who, when the game warden ordered him to stop digging clams, said, "I been eating these clams for eighty years and ain't nobody gonna stop me now."

"And?"

"The warden says, 'Okay, but if you die, don't say I didn't warn you.' If you ask me," muses Richard, "lots more people die in traffic than the red tide. How many you suppose ever died of it on the East Coast—two or three, maybe? No one around here, I betcha. Nope, ain't never heard of a one."

"Then why is the radio saying—?"

"Beats me. I'll say one thing—those warnings are for the whole coast—Maine, Massachusetts, Connecticut—like there ain't no difference between one spot and another. But I don't see no red on that water out there, do you? They see it one place, they close down the whole coast. Who knows, maybe they're trying to drive up the price of clams, like they done with oil, saying there was a shortage, when everyone knows now there weren't no shortage."

By the time Richard leaves I'm reassured. I trust him far more than I do the government. But out on the deck as the sun begins to set I see the water of the cove turn a deep shimmering red, and my doubts return. Is it the sunset or a different, a deadly red? How can I tell? I decide to go with faith, so when the tide's right I pick six mussels (instead of my usual twelve) and eat my soup as if it's my last supper. It feels like shooting the rapids and tastes as delicious as ever—though that evening I watch for headache, altered vision.

The next morning I'm still alive. And the water is again perfectly blue, the gulls and cormorants fishing as always. Shellfish, I begin to think, may simply be one of the hazards of island life, like traffic risks or muggings in the city. The crime and traffic statistics published in the papers are no doubt true—still, only the cripplingly timid or paranoid stop going out. Richard's statistics are even more telling: not one shellfish death or illness in his memory. Based on that, and my own experience, I decide to look both ways, and if a mussel looks, smells, and tastes okay I'll eat it.

My mailbox stands just beyond South Beach where the dirt road begins—a whole new world. Pineapple weed, a compact quarter-inch flower that, incredibly, looks and smells exactly like a miniature pineapple, grows just before the tiny stream that separates the beach from the road; across the stream is a grove of versatile cattails. On my frequent mail runs I encounter everything from post-storm jellyfish and sea gulls' bones to witty driftwood sculptures and Frisbee-throwing day-trippers. Then one day a large ferocious-sounding dog stands on the beach in wait for me.

The dog is running a wide but diminishing circle around me, his mouth open, barking, slavering. "Down, Dragon!" cries his owner sharply—and to me: "He'll stop barking as soon as you've gone past." Still, fear grips me, compounded by self-disgust. Having triumphed over my dread of the hacker and even of red tide, why am I still dragging around this useless fear of dogs that's hounded me since childhood? I know it's fear far more than dogs that injures me; for all my carrying-on, I've never once been bitten. It's time to drop it—but how? "What can a man do to overcome fear?" asks Carlos Castaneda of his teacher, the Yaqui Indian sorcerer don Juan, for whom fear is "the first enemy of a man of knowledge." "The answer is very simple," says don Juan. "He must not run away. He must defy his fear, and in spite of it he must take the next step in learning, and the next. He must be fully afraid, and yet he must not stop. That is the rule! And a moment will come when his first enemy retreats . . ."

That night I struggle to remember that fear is a burden, a malady, a body-snatcher that can drive one mad. I count the fears I've overcome, reliving the triumph of my first dive from the high board, first arrest, first speech before strangers, first solo summer on the nubble—all of which from this side of the divide seem like nothing at all, certainly nothing to claim any credit for.

By the next morning my resolve is firm enough to carry me past that barking dog without my slowing down or tensing up. Willing my heart to beat normally, I defy the urge to turn back or freeze or cry out. The dog circles me, barking as before, but somehow I manage to ignore him as if I were fearless—and suddenly, miraculously, like Amy spotting a four-leaf clover, I am!

But there's always another fear to take up the torch. In my mailbox an ominous yellow slip announces a piece of registered mail awaiting my signature at the post office. I examine it for clues. Internal Revenue? Jury call? Exercising discipline, I wait until my regular Saturday walk across the island to the pay phone before stopping in to sign for a fat packet from a New York law firm. I scan the cover of an official document in a blue binding and see I'm being sued —for divorce.

I manage to chatter with the postmaster even though my heart is thumping against my ribs. Why has Jerry chosen this method to break with me, this silent assault? It feels like a kick in the stomach or a blow with a baseball bat. I stuff the papers back into their envelope and quickly press them into my bag to read later, alone, when I can think.

By the time I've collapsed on the beach to read the opaque document, a fog so thick it shrouds my feet has engulfed this side of the island. Mainland anxieties clog my throat, bleating foghorns fill my ears. Through the fog I see my married lives unfold before me, from the opening credits played over a hasty wedding in the Temple chapel—I, a child bride at twenty, still wrapped in baby fat, in a blue beaded dress; my young husband fussing with his first boutonniere, while the rabbi's wife, a soprano, sings "Oh, Promise Me," accompanying herself on the organ—and rapidly my narrative unfolds through all the messy intervening years.

How quickly we all rushed to marry in that decade after the war, needing to rebuild the homes, replace the dead.

Better safe than sorry, we said, marching to the altar, two by two. Even though I had secretly fantasized freedom, making practice runs in ever expanding circles by scheming for summer jobs away from home and applying to a distant college no one in my family had ever heard of, insisting on a single in the dorm, I buckled under when the moment came. Safe *and* sorry.

Five years later I created a scandal by becoming the only divorced woman in the family on either side (though not for long). Alone for a moment at twenty-six, in a panic I married again. "We shall exchange one tyranny for another. And the second tyranny will be worse than the first because between the two there will have been the lost chance of freedom," writes John Berger in a passage as yet unwritten at the time I needed it. My second husband was a charming sturdy bearlike man I barely had time to know in the few customary months between names. A promising provider, a family man. Still cherishing fantasies of freedom, I waited till the last permissible moment to push my firstborn into the world—just under the wire on the eve of thirty. First Stevie, a boy, and after I had nursed him for a decent interval, Amy, a girl. Captivating creatures, precious principals of my new life, bubbling fountains of vivacity.

But you can't outsmart desire, that nimble dancer always two steps ahead of you, twirling around to confront you with a sly grin. Alone no more, compounded forever, helplessly hooked into this world, I relinquished unity. For trinity, for security. *Security?* Wouldn't I have been safer alone, dependent on no one, no one dependent on me? But those babies in my arms, at my breast, clutching my hands, pulling on my hair, teething on my heart, tugging at my sleeve, one child in the stroller, one helping me push, ceaselessly absorbing all my loyalty and love—those children redefined every question of bravery, courage, and independence. For now my safety—*our* safety—and destiny were in someone else's hands. With him we rose, with him we fell. The safety people seek in numbers turned into danger—the more of us, the greater the danger. I surrendered to multiplicity, walled us up in the fortress that is the family, and settled down, down, down.

Once the family was in place, my sandy-haired husband, who'd been lazily devoted to me, reached up and out to grab the world—"for the family," he said. He had a scheme to get rich. He'd don a fancy suit, borrow money from his brother-in-law, build a company. "We can't lose," he said. The lawyer, the accountant, the tax man, the banker all agreed. "Now all they need is your signature on the loan papers—"

"My signature? Why mine?"

"Just a formality. They always insist on the wife's signature."

"But I don't have anything—just the little I earn at my freelance jobs. Why should anyone want my signature?"

"They want to insure that if I go bankrupt I can't just slip everything to you."

"Everything? Like what?"

He was losing patience, getting ready to bully me . . . and Amy was waking up. "Like—everything. The furniture, the car, The cabin . . ." He waved his hand vaguely at the world. "People put the titles in their wives' names to keep the property out of the assets."

"Don't give me any titles, then." Mrs. and Mommy are enough. "If you go bankrupt my earnings will be our only fallback. I can't possibly sign."

"They won't give me the loan if you don't sign. We need this business. It's for us."

We? Us? Never had I felt more alone or exposed. Having recently reread the fairy tales as bedtime stories for Stevie,

I knew better than to sign away the future. Rumpelstiltskin, the Miller's Daughter, Sleeping Beauty—they all warn about just this. "This is your business, not mine. I don't need it. I don't want it. After you start up this business we'll see even less of you than we do now. All I want is for us to eat together sometimes as a family."

His head slightly lowered, brow furrowed, shoulders hunched, left foot pawed the ground. "Are you going to sign?"

I was terrified, but not for one instant did I hesitate. "No. I can't."

Thus the fog rolled in. He opened his business anyway, withdrew from us. We saw him as seldom as I feared. The end of our adventure, the death of love. Each morning he'd leave us to take his breakfast in a diner where he'd be able to read the *Times* uninterrupted, while we began our day in the kitchen. Stevie banged his spoon on the high chair. The baby grasped her right foot in her left hand and in her excitement dropped her bottle. Let him go, then. Never mind, never mind . . .

The Sixties, the Seventies, those fermenting years bubbled up around us, intoxicating the young, frightening the old, seducing the almost free. They swirled about us, rumbling overhead and underfoot, then drifted past. Through war and peace we stood hand in hand, looking up, riveted, my children and I. Look! we cried, pointing upward, look! Brightly colored balloons, feathers, pigeons, distant jets, clouds glided by, music harsh and lush filled the air, drums beat the rhythms for dancing or marching mobs, clowns cavorted, Polaroids, microchips, hot tubs came to pass, people pulled themselves up by the roots and floated on by, gauzy, flowery, hairy, spacy, ambitious, bicoastal.

This spectacle usually took place in a city park. Outside were traffic jams. Gridlock trapped us while WALK–DON'T

WALK flashed endlessly through cycles of green and red. Virtuously we waited together to cross the streets in safety, until one day I crossed the children from the living-room window, then before I could stop them they were crossing on their own, and I, when there was no one to see my bad example, began reenacting the anarchic jaywalk of my once carefree youth, rushing back into the mad traffic of our high-voltage times. History exploded. I started to write. The movement was born. I published. And when Jerry's business collapsed, and we needed my earnings to live, I cried: You see? You see?

After that, his jobs carried him ever farther away, leaving me to be both parents—each one unable to imagine my life without the children, our dinners together, our elaborate projects, our afternoon walks, our late-night talks. And then one day—just like this, in the middle of a paragraph—they too were gone. First Stevie departed, leaving me and Amy to cry over his empty place at table, then Amy followed him. And they who as children had always called me Mommy began addressing me as Mother. And there was no more need to be married.

STILL, as I sit in the fog reading the disturbing papers, I'm overcome by fear and misgivings. Worse than the brutality of the legal language, the outrageous accusations, the raw hostility, is this precipitate assault on my tranquillity. To preserve it I'll have to battle for it—and thus destroy it. (I have sixty days to hire a lawyer and respond.) Reason tells me that with the children grown I should welcome this divorce. I've been imagining it for years; without it I can never be wholly free. But fear is hardly rational, as I've discovered by sometimes routing it so easily.

I return the papers to their envelope and start back up

toward the cabin. Jerry bought this place over my veto and holds the title. Now in the shroud of mist I see only the gloomy prospect of losing it.

All night long I lie awake replaying the papers. The next morning the fog is even thicker, and a faint green mold begins to bloom on the deck and spread over the steps. The railing drips. The songbirds stop singing. For most of the day I stay inside reciting my new mantra, *Shun attachment*, writing it on little slips of paper that I post around the cabin in select spots—over my desk, beside the bed. But the mantra serves mainly to remind me of my deep attachment to the nubble.

THAT night I'm savoring a mussel stew when I chomp down on something hard. In the fog, I had gathered my mussels from nearby Skip Stone Cove, where they lay half buried in sandy muck. And though I took my usual precaution of cooking them in a separate pot and straining the broth before adding it to the stew, something hard and gritty has slipped through. I just hope I haven't broken a tooth. I isolate the foreign object with my tongue and work it out with my fingers into the palm of my hand, where I can study it. A tiny luminous sphere of an almost translucent white, it looks like nothing so much as . . . a pearl!

Can it be? Do mussels make pearls? Soon I find another. And another. Unmistakably, there are pearls in my soup. And a new, peculiar trade-off: precious pearls versus cracked fillings or broken teeth if I'm not extremely alert. I lay my treasures in an empty mussel shell and concentrate exclusively on texture as I attend to this novel meal, bite by promising bite.

The next day I'm back in Skip Stone Cove in the fog, upending rocks for hidden treasure; at dinner that night again pearls fall from my lips—sometimes three, four, even five from a single mussel. Is it something in the mucky habitat? The time of year? My books are silent on the question. All I know is that I never before found a pearl, while tonight all but two mussels have them.

I'm so excited by my new discovery that the next morning when the foggy curtain rolls back, opening vast vistas halfway to France, I rejoice that I'm now free to pick my mussels anywhere to advance my investigations. From the deck the horizon seems farther, the air clearer than I've ever seen them, revealing islands I never guessed were there. On the water each ripple stands erect as it rides the waves, poised for an instant before falling in. "Sometimes ocean people are given to understand the newness and oldness of the world; then all morning they try to keep that boundless joy like a little sun inside their chests," writes Maxine Hong Kingston. In the brush warblers and finches are trilling again; raspberries glisten; the gulls are laughing. My divorce is hundreds of miles away.

I keep collecting pearls until soon I have so many—translucent and opaque; single, double, triple; round and oblong; white, black, gray, purple, blue, silver, cream, eggshell—that I begin enclosing in my letters small gifts of mussel pearls wrapped in tiny new envelopes I construct from scraps of old ones. I send them to my children and friends who mostly write back, as I once exclaimed myself, "I never knew mussels could make pearls!"

One morning a franked, official letter from the state capital stares out at me from inside my mailbox like a coiled snake. Panic returns; I've turned mail-shy. My fingers tremble as I rip open the envelope and continue to tremble even when I see with relief that the letter has nothing to do with divorce but is a reply to a query I sent to the Department of Fisheries. Pearls are formed by secretions of mother-of-pearl, the iridescent nacreous material that lines the inside of mollusk shells, around the dead body of a tiny parasite that has penetrated the mollusk's tissue. The particular larva around which a mussel pearl forms lives in its adult stage in the eider duck.

The eider duck? Even as I round the point taking this in, a long flotilla of eider glides into view behind the Shmoos, bearing on their bodies tons of down and the seeds of a thousand future pearls. I count a hundred eighty-five moving along the shore in a long column, three or four bodies deep. Above their heads a flock of twenty semi-palmated sandpipers swoops in to execute a fast balletic turn, while higher still, over the sandpipers, half a dozen herring gulls pump steadily toward shore. How gracefully each flock occupies its own distinct altitude without crowding one another—managing so much better than Jerry and I, despite our best intentions. As I walk along contemplating these intricate harmonies, I see my solitude as a luminous pearl that has formed around the dead body of my marriage.

SEVEN

THE postcard from Margaret Flood gave no arrival date, but it wouldn't be a day too soon. Since I sent her a map and a ferry schedule I'd been watching for her. I need her help with my divorce.

Seeing a small figure moving slowly across the beach, I rush to the edge of the deck. Before I can see her face I recognize the long silver hair, the flowing red garment, the shopping bag in each hand. (A great adapter, Margaret always travels light, supplementing from local thrift shops.) I wave my arms and hoot, then take the steps two at a time and sprint across the sand. I lift her small body off the ground and twirl her—first human touch in months. After I set her down she continues to twirl like a dervish, her arms spread to the sky. "Here I am," she announces in a high melodious voice.

Though I sometimes jokingly refer to Margaret as my guru, we've seen each other seldom over the years, and only in the city; she's never before been to Maine. Now we're both suddenly struck by the utter implausibility of either of us, much less both of us together, winding up on this remote northern beach; and before we've even reached the cabin we're already shrieking our joy and laughing like mad. Two mad ladies in tennis shoes.

"My-oh-my-oh-my," exclaims Margaret quaintly, taking in every large and tiny thing. I trail behind her through the cabin, looking through her eyes. "Holy moly!" she says, picking up a large bleached spiral shell.

"Moon shell," I report, and tell her how it can be found only when the new moon or full moon pulls the tide far enough back from shore, and how delicious are pounded moon-shell steaks. We stop in front of the three shelves I've hung on the wall outside the storeroom, their animal, vegetable, mineral contents arranged shelf by shelf. "What's this?" she asks like a child. "What's this?"

One would never guess, seeing this pixie woman examining a feather, that her true vocation is gadfly and general provocateur whose free, sometimes shocking behavior and ideas, however sweetly expressed, can goad her adversaries to sputtering rage. "It doesn't surprise me when they explode," she explains. "If someone's really sleeping soundly, you know how it feels to be woken up." To me, she's simply the most interesting person I know, daringly rolling an idea along the thin edge between outrageous and enlightening, like a child skipping alongside a hoop, hitting it with a stick. She has six children and ten grandchildren, plus two lovers her children's age, whose doings endlessly intrigue me.

In the kitchen she stops before the rusty old Queen Atlantic and puzzles over the sandstone potatoes and bread I once found in the cove and arranged on top of the stove like real food. "Touch them," I urge. She runs her hands over the perfect image of a crusty brown loaf and lifts the heavy stone potatoes, then breaks into a grin, revealing several missing teeth. Otherwise, the diminutive bones of her wiry frame seem strong enough, even supple, as she glides around the cabin, stopping to appreciate each shell, rock, bird's nest, each piece of driftwood or glass, fungus or fern. She bends over the table to sniff a bouquet I picked fresh that morning and arranged in a mustard jar. Wild pink roses, purple nightshade, daisies, and meadowsweet. She closes her eyes and inhales.

I settle Margaret in the corner room that was always the children's, placing her shopping bags on one of the two iron cots, then carry in the flowers. She lifts a bottle and a book out of her bag to offer me. Chardonnay and the *Tao Te Ching*—the second copy of the *Tao* she's given me. Is she losing her memory as well as her teeth? A pang of protection crosses a wave of pure love—the same love I felt the moment I met her. She plops down on the empty cot and lifts a curtain to peer out the window. Past the clothesline strung between two posts on the back deck, past the bramble brush dotted with wildflowers, past the necklace of gulls circling Marsh Island, and on to the sea.

As I hover nearby watching her, into my mind pops the Watchbird, an image that appeared every month in *The Ladies' Home Journal* when I was growing up. A cartoon drawing of a youth committing some moral or social breach, with a large bird nearby observing him, and the ominous caption: "This is a Watchbird watching a ———. This is a Watchbird watching you. Were you a ——— this month?" Fill in with a different sin or gaffe for each month. The Watchbird is what I came to this island to escape. Impossible to do immersed in society, but almost easy here. For some people, their Watchbird flaps around their head, peering over a shoulder to see what they're reading, counting their calories and cholesterol as they eat, peeking into their ears and eyes to catch them thinking, monitoring their ambitions and desires. But my Watchbird finds isolation boring; once I'm here alone, I'm free. I back quietly out of the room to leave Margaret all the space she needs.

• • •

"READY for the grand tour?" I ask, tossing Margaret some zoris and a pair of old jeans that I find in the trunk. We set off clockwise around the nubble to pick our dinner. At the bottom of the stairs we stop to sample beach peas—as sweet as garden peas, only half the size. In the cove I point out sand hoppers, brine shrimp, hermit crabs that live in any old empty shell, wandering from house to house—just like Margaret who, lacking a permanent address, might be regarded as homeless but for her large extended family constantly vying for her healing visits. A specialist in crisis intervention, besides counseling her friends and family, she has nursed earthquake victims in Guatemala, marched with the Madres in Nicaragua, lectured in free schools and prisons on several continents, ministered to the dying and the newborn.

We scramble up the jagged rock outcroppings at the tip of the nubble over to the ocean side, and on down to my waving seaweed gardens. Here twice a day the ebbing tide uncovers an entire vegetable world: purple dulse, kelp, tender tangle, emerald-green sea lettuce (a handful of which I pick for our salad), and curly Irish moss (ditto for our paella). Margaret has bought and sold dried seaweeds in the health-food stores where she sometimes works but has never had them fresh. I hand her a few spaghetti strands of arame, my favorite snack, crunchy as cucumber with a salty tang, to munch along the way.

We round a bend to Dedgers, where heavy surf crashes against the rocks, sending rainbows of salt spray into the air. Centuries of spray have pitted the shale to lacy cheese and carved out giant footprints. We detour to the Bathtub, a deep semi-enclosed hollow in the rocks where heavy stones trapped in the pit tumble in the roiling surf, polishing the chasm walls and one another as smooth as glass. At the top of the slippery wall are two natural thrones with rounded seats where the children sat as toddlers while I soaped them up and afterward rinsed off by splashing around in the pool while the tide ran out. I see them still: bending over the smooth cobbles, green, purple, white, and black, sorting, separating, counting, polishing—just like Margaret, who has slipped off her jeans to try out the thrones and climb down into the tub.

As she sorts through stones, I study her aging body to see what's coming next for me. Her small breasts sag gracefully, her smooth legs are brown and firm. As she tips her face toward the sun it's as if time has forgotten her.

Like mine, Margaret's second act began at fifty. One day, when the last of her children was grown, she packed a bag and, leaving everything behind, including house, pool, and philandering husband, hitchhiked down to Mexico with no resources but what came to her through serendipity. There she took a new name, studied midwifery, and joined a birthing community just in time to deliver her first grandchild. That was more than a dozen years ago. I met her soon after, on one of her brief New York visits, when we found ourselves side by side standing on a line to peer through a plastic speculum at a volunteer's cervix—a piece of every woman's anatomy that many of us were seeing for the first time. It felt challenging and risky, like prospecting for gold. That meeting had been organized to learn "menstrual extraction," a new technique for early abortion that women could perform on one another in defiance of the legal and medical professions' proclaimed monopoly of our bodies. Margaret radiated such radical free spirit, such electricity, that I fell directly in love. That I was a hard-nosed East Coast activist, she an antic hippie mystic (eventual veteran of mystic schools in Scotland, England, Iran, and India) made no difference at all. I took her home from the meeting and kept her with me for a night and a day, until she had to leave the city. We never even bothered to sleep.

Finally we arrive at my exhibition mussel bed just after the tide has turned. The pool is clear and still, filled with perfect specimens. Margaret digs in. We take two dozen blues and a dozen of their predators, the small green crabs that are never far away. I show her how to spot a crab beneath the rockweed and grab it from behind without getting pinched, grasping the widest points of its carapace between thumb and forefinger.

When we've reached our quota we pick our way back to dry land, balancing on slippery rocks, seeking those covered with barnacles for better traction. I show her the erosion that's gradually toppling this bit of nubble into the sea. "In a hundred years this may all be gone," I lament.

Margaret chuckles: "So will you."

Crossing the nubble's neck to Singing Sand Beach, I introduce her to the salad bar. We pick orach and lamb's-quarters, yellow dock and charlock, sea rocket and the delicate red fruit of the strawberry goosefoot. Ever game, she sniffs each new specimen I hand her and munches thoughtfully, head tipped to one side, and slowly repeats its name. When our buckets are full, we top the tour with a skidding riff of singing sand.

We sit on canvas chairs on the front deck—I in the shade of the overhang, she facing the sun—and settle down to talk. After months of near silence, broken only by Saturday-morning phone calls and occasional exchanges with an islander, I want to gorge on conversation. Not chitchat, for which the purity of silence has only made me more unfit, but the intimate life-and-death talk we always have. Having exchanged no more than a few letters and phone calls (though much telepathy) between our rare visits, we've barely begun to tell our stories or explore each other's lives. Though we share passions, desires, and doubts, we are constantly startled by how differently we approach and express them. Until now, at least, we've been yin/yang soul mates: she mystical, I political; she unifying, I analyzing; she spiritual, I historical; she sociable, I solitary; she the Buddha's advocate, I the devil's. Now I want to reconcile our differences, learn her ways.

I fill tall glasses with an infusion I've made from the astringent red cluster flowers of staghorn sumac, sweetened with honey—a kind of mock pink lemonade. Then I raise my glass and offer a libation to my beloved.

She sniffs, tastes, swallows, smiles—and as we sip the potion the conversation levitates, carrying us out of ourselves into a world of leaps and loops, puzzles and conundrums. My new discoveries, so fragile and hard to name, gain substance through Margaret's understanding, which often yields a perfect parable. Her mind, tuned to essential questions, sees connections so clearly that she can reach all the way around the most distant digression and draw it like a shy child into the center of the conversation, making it fit right in, rendering even the most casual offhand remark pertinent, consequential, apropos. If in my excitement I sometimes, apologizing, interrupt her, she graciously reminds me that it's impossible to interrupt her, since everything we say is connected. And indeed, that's the pleasure of this conversation—the way it stretches and expands till it explodes in revelation.

All afternoon we soar, leaving our separate egos below on the deck, growing greater than the sum of our parts until the last stray picnicker has left the beach, the last few boats have set sail from the cove, and suddenly it's dinnertime. So soon! Margaret stretches her back, shakes out her legs, pushes back her silver hair, and slapping her hands together like cymbals says, "Since this discussion is endless, we might as well end it here."

AFTER half a lifetime of cooking several meals a day for a family of eight, Margaret cozies right up in my kitchen. I can see that she too considers cooking an outlet for creative expression—like music or dance. Work and worship are one to her. Since she left her husband's house she has earned her keep variously as a cook, vender, salesclerk, housepainter, floor scrubber, teacher, adviser, companion, comforter—to the battered, the homeless, the elderly. When her Social Security check fails to last the month, or whenever her help is needed, she takes another job.

We browse through my cookbooks, perusing recipes, not as formulas or prescriptions but as hints and inspirations for impromptu inventions. Then we assemble our ingredients, take up our instruments—our knives, mixing bowls, measures—and begin. We slice green apples from my tree, scrub mussels and crabs, extract periwinkles from their shells. Margaret mixes dough and rolls out the pie shell; I measure the rice and season the mussel broth with juniper, bayberry, Irish moss, and a dash of wine. Then we build our salad, sampling each wild thing as we add it to the big wooden bowl. On top of the greens I sprinkle some of the goosefoot "strawberries" and a fistful of yellow charlock blossoms, bright and mustardy. Presentation counts.

Margaret reports a recent newspaper headline declaring food flowers soigné. In certain fancy restaurants, the chefs have begun to decorate their salads with pansies, violets, or nasturtiums, though hardly anyone actually eats them. This amuses us, since people are glad to eat such flowers as cauliflower, broccoli, and artichokes. While the pie bakes and the rice steams, we do a quick survey of the parts of plants, noting that people eat all of them in some form or other: roots (carrot), sprouts (bean), leaves (cabbage), stalks (celery), pods (pepper), seeds, fruits, nuts. "Even bark," observes Margaret, naming cinnamon. "Even stamens," I add, naming saffron. Yet, for any given plant, we generally eat only the single choice part we've been taught to eat, and throw the rest away.

"That's one of the reasons I love weeds," I tell her. "I can experiment with every part since there are no conventions about which parts are edible."

Margaret laughs. "Presumably, they're all inedible."

I describe cattails, edible from their shoots, that have the sweetness of corn and the texture of asparagus, down to their roastable roots and up to their powdery pollen, that can double as a kind of flour. And curly dock, the potherb with the long citric-flavored leaves, which becomes an entirely new resource when it goes to seed, producing forty thousand seeds I can harvest simply by sliding the stalks through my fist, then fold into muffins and grains.

Margaret describes the practice of her third son, Michael, a poet, who questions the very concept of garbage. As confidante to six offspring, all children of the Sixties, she knows whole worlds unfamiliar to me. Among her children and their mates are a teacher, dancer, poet, nurse, doctor, social worker, carpenter, waiter, banker, singer—all of whom she visits regularly, using cut-rate senior-citizen fares. I call her the holy mother. "Michael would never violate a potato by peeling it," she says, or throw out the tops of carrots, leaves of celery, stems of parsley, pods of peas, skins of fruits.

This idea appeals to me instantly. What is garbage, after all, but the part of food we throw away? Besides the indigestible, like bones and shells or chokes and cobs, it includes the used, like cooking liquids and leftovers; the old, like the sour, moldy, hard, soft, separated, stale; and the merely unappealing, like untraditional or discolored parts—the peelings, tips, stems, flowers, fat, viscera, skin of the very foods we prize. But most of these are somewhere used for food. Before World War II, no conscientious housewife could bear to throw cooking liquids away. When yeast starters got old and oversour she knew how to "freshen" them—by adding to them, not throwing them out. Bones and shells enhanced stocks; sour dairy products were transformed into cheeses; stale bread became bread crumbs and croutons, peels and rinds became chutneys and candies; and even today all over the world what can't be utilized fresh is often preserved simply by drying, including a vast variety of fruits, flowers, beans, fungi, even fish, shellfish, and meats. Not that every part of every plant is edible—rhubarb, for example, has toxic leaves—or equally easy to prepare. But the parts that can't be eaten can be turned into compost.

"Remember George Washington Carver, who invented a thousand ways to use a peanut and a hundred ways to use a yam?" asks Margaret.

"Or us," I offer, "with our score of ways to eat an apple." (Years later, when papayas the size of footballs ripen every day behind my rented Honolulu house, I'll learn as many ways to eat papaya: raw, cooked, marinated, preserved, green, ripe—each in a dozen variations. The same with apricots in Santa Fe.)

MARGARET tells a joke: "Man comes home from work, finds his wife stretched out ill on the sofa. What's the matter, honey, he says, aren't you feeling well? I'm afraid not, says the wife, I must be coming down with something, and I haven't got our dinner yet. Don't worry, says the husband, I'll get the dinner, you just stay right there and rest. He goes into the kitchen, bangs some cupboards, then returns to the living room. Honey, excuse me, I looked for the dinner but I couldn't find it. Where do you keep it?"

WE set the table on the front deck facing the empty beach. Margaret pours the wine, I bring out the steaming paella, dense with mussels and periwinkles, dotted with red crabs and tiny peas. On the floor I place a pot for the empty shells, which we'll return to the sea. Our gorgeous salad shines in the wooden bowl, with its array of red, yellow, and vari-colored greens. When we're finally settled, Margaret takes my hands in hers and looks me intently in the eyes. Her bright hazel eyes, usually so animated, are serene. From our steaming plates rise invisible vapors, wafting delicious aromas to our nostrils, and I feel like a birthday child wishing on candles. We wish. Then we click our glasses, pick up our forks, and fall to.

We eat more slowly than usual, drawing out the meal, savoring each body, leaf, and pea with the same patience and regard we used to gather and prepare them. Margaret eats without a trace of squeamishness, concentrating on each new ingredient as if it were one of her children needing a dose of undivided attention. Not even her missing teeth (lost when the first dentist she visited in years scraped off the calculus and tartar buildup which, she speculates, had been functioning as cement to hold the teeth in place) prevent her chewing up the little crabs, legs and all.

The sun disappears behind the ridge and twilight arrives, turning the sky the color of ripe berries. We had intended to enjoy the sunset, but we are so absorbed in our gustatory pleasures that we never stop to notice it; and now, as we down our melting apple pie, the mosquitoes gather ("mosquito rush hour," Stevie used to call dusk), joining the feast to feed on us. Margaret brushes them from her face, I swat at my legs and arms until we are forced to pile our dishes on a tray and move indoors.

Inside it's already dark. We'll leave the dishes for morning. I light the lamps; Margaret lights a joint, though we're already high on the meal. In the glow of lamplight the deer head mounted over the door, the hand-carved lobster buoys hanging from the high center beam, the twelve-sided table at which we sit sipping tea—all take on a new particularity. Margaret reminds me that just as my generation deplored the pitiless glare of fluorescent light, so when incandescent electric lights were introduced many people bemoaned their harsh steady blaze compared to the warm flicker of gaslight—as, I suppose, earlier, some regretted the passing of candlelight. For a while we savor the light. But soon we are again deep in our conversation, exploring the paradoxes that rule the nubble like perverse commandments: *yield and overcome, bend and be straight, empty and be full,* as the *Tao* says. A cricket joins in, one of the lamps hums a low hum, but what I want to hear is Margaret. Our talk is as nourishing as food, as satisfying as sleep. I can't seem to get enough of it.

Evidently, neither can she, for even after we finally go to bed we continue our exchange, laughing and shouting through the night across the partitions that separate the rooms.

The next morning over breakfast on the shady back deck we're at it again. And each subsequent morning. Our breakfast talk is often sober, touching my divorce. Who needs a lawyer with Margaret to explain how "divorce is simply the continuation of marriage by other means." Having had six children to console when her marriage ended, she comforts me as I weep over my two, whose sadness and anger leak through the wires when I phone them on Saturdays.

When the dishes are done we take vows of silence. Margaret heads for the rocks, leaving me alone with my notebooks and books until lunchtime or low tide, whichever comes first. We forage for an hour at low tide, maybe lunch on the beach. Then she disappears again (to where, I never know) until, haloed in backlight from the setting sun, she climbs the stairs to resume our culinary experiments and our conversation. On other days, if it seems right, after lunch we toss our resolutions into the air and catch whatever comes floating down—a clam dig, a swim, a berry expedition, sand sculpting, a walk to the dump. Because, what the hell, we're both over fifty, alone, and free.

THE dump is the closest thing to entertainment we have on the island, so one afternoon after lunch we tie up the bag filled mainly with beach trash we've collected, load it into the shopping cart, and set off for the source of the pink piano, a 1924 Fannie Farmer cookbook, and some of my favorite things.

Located across a narrow road from the one-room former schoolhouse, the dump sits on a plot of sandy earth flanked by pine and birch woods and backed by a ravine. Periodically a bulldozer clears the plot by pushing some of the bulkier refuse into the ravine. Though for generations this dump has been an invaluable resource for searchers and dreamers, often providing the necessary missing item, eventually all this will change. Stringent rules will be enacted, large solid waste will be barged to the mainland, one day the dump will be closed. Even in this year of Margaret's first visit, I warn her that the place is no longer the dump it used to be when people frugally "recycled" their discards as a matter of course by depositing them here for others to salvage.

A dozen gulls are lined up on the ridge of the schoolhouse

roof with such perfect spacing that they look like stone decorations. When we park the shopping cart and dump our bag, they swoop down to investigate. Between the gulls, the cats, and the field mice, even the garbage gets recycled, leaving the dump fairly clean and odor-free—like our outhouse, Margaret observes.

A skinny half-grown gray tiger with huge eyes and long white whiskers ventures toward us, then attaches itself to Margaret, circling her and rubbing against her legs. As she bends down to pet it, more cats appear, slinking out of overturned refrigerators and sprung mattresses, climbing through the legs of broken chairs, stalking along the branches of felled trees. The place is overrun with feral cats, progeny of pets abandoned at summer's end. I explain that Bob the cat man, a ponytailed carpenter, cares for them, preparing their food and transporting them to a Portland vet for vasectomies and hysterectomies. And not only Bob; each October the island's winter residents hold a fund-raising party to support Bob's efforts.

We walk through this user-friendly dump, exchanging salvage stories. Children of World War II, we developed character by saving everything from newspapers and magazines, which we collected house-to-house in our red wagons for school paper sales, to used clothing for Russian relief, to rubber bands and tinfoil we rolled into balls, to every sort of metal scrap including cans, tubes, razor blades, and large appliances. We competed by school, grade, class, and individual to see who could save the most. When my brother donated his bicycle to the large scrap drive, I donated our swing set to outdo him. Pass-it-on and hand-me-down were axioms of public service back when luxuries were in short supply and frugality was virtue. Our clever fathers straightened nails and got multiple shaves from a single blade; our resourceful mothers rendered cooking fat, let down our hems, mended our socks, saved every last sliver of soap. But then the war ended, and in the extravagant, profligate postwar years—right up until yesterday—the impulse to conserve was relabeled "cheap" or "stingy," and the mantle of respect passed to the prodigal squanderers and big spenders.

Margaret spots someone's ancestor in an ornate oval frame. The glass is cracked and the wood chipped, but she's intrigued. The ancestor's face is severe; her high bosom is tightly encased in a tucked blouse with leg-o'-mutton sleeves. "Why do you suppose anyone would throw out a thing like this?" she muses, holding the picture at arm's length.

The essential dump question: Why is one person's trash another one's treasure? Like my hand-painted trays, oak drawer, glass doorknobs, old toys, books, walnut medicine cabinet. Or the more practical nuts and bolts, pots and lids, bowls and buckets. Because there's only one store and nothing much to buy. Because the children have grown up and gone away. Because it's difficult to transport things on and off an island. "You can read the history of the island right here," I suggest. "Once Mat Burns found a perfect cast-iron stove with all its parts and some lovely wooden cabinets when someone modernized their kitchen."

By the time our shopping cart is full, we've salvaged: a gaily painted watering can which, though it may no longer hold water, will make an ideal container for dried flowers, a broken birdhouse I plan to fix, a wicker basket, a straw hat, and several charming playing cards, circa 1950, picturing a pair of Spanish dancers, castanets held high, disdainful heads thrown proudly back.

I take us up a secret path behind the school, lined with high bushes dripping with blueberries. When we've eaten our fill and our tongues have turned blue, Margaret exclaims that everything one might want or need is right here.

I've often had a similar thought, especially regarding food. But everything? "You don't mean *everything*," I say, feeling scrappy.

"Yes I do—with the right attitude. Once you understand there's no garbage or junk or weeds."

I consider. Given that my greatest pleasure lies in making do, that what I most crave is nothing, my experience backs her up. But reason rebels. "What about movies?" I challenge, confident I've hit on something. In the city I usually saw at least one film a week, choosing from a huge menu.

"Even movies," replies Margaret.

As I raise a dubious eyebrow, Margaret grows bold. "I promise you that whenever you have the urge to go to a movie, there'll be something you really want to see showing in Portland, just a ferry ride away."

I'm doubtful—particularly in face of her certitude. "But Portland has so few theaters to choose from," I counter.

"You can only see one movie at a time."

"What if I've seen everything that's showing?"

"Not likely, living way out here, is it?"

She has a point. Still, we continue to go round and round, my irritation mounting at every turn, even though I know I usually learn less by opposing Margaret than by trying to understand her. Indeed, often our conversations are like dancing: sometimes we tango through our talk, gliding along in tandem; sometimes we march briskly, side by side, then make high running leaps to unexpected conclusions; sometimes we sway together in place like monks at prayer, or twirl like whirling dervishes. If we come to an impasse, either of us might respectfully call *po*—a friendly, consoling syllable, connected to *po*ssibly, *po*tential, *po*lite, and *po*etry, meaning: I have listened to what you are saying and neither agree nor disagree. But occasionally a word, a definition, an attitude looms like a weapon between us, threatening to destroy the conversation. Our voices tighten, sharpen. Instead of enlarging or refining our paradoxes, we start pulling them apart, taking sides. Our separate egos muscle in between us—contentious, sparring adversaries; and even if I can see her side, I cling stubbornly to my own. Such a futile display—because if I really believed in my opinion, I wouldn't have to defend it so churlishly; I could let it glow like truth in its own light. But I've identified myself with this flawed and partial thing, defending it simply because I've called it mine. And even if I want to drop it and open my mind again, with Margaret's immense presence now filling the space like weather, I can't find room to let go.

Ah, but Margaret can. Just before we go too far she'll usually rescue the conversation by sliding it onto another plane, or telling a pertinent joke, or, in extremis, repeating, "This subject is endless, so why not end it here."

This time she excuses herself to go pee in the bushes. While she's gone I see her point: even when a film I want to see is showing in Portland, one I regret having missed in New York, I'd still rather not leave the island. Someday I might—but so far I've invariably preferred to stay put.

"It turns out you may be right," I grudgingly admit when she returns. "Because when it comes down to it I don't want to go to any movie if I can be here instead. But"—not yet ready to concede—"suppose I did?"

Margaret guffaws. "That's like saying, suppose you wanted a Mercedes."

"Well, suppose I did?"

"The point is, you don't. And if you really did want a Mercedes you certainly wouldn't be living like *this*, you wouldn't be *here*, where you have no more chance than a pig in a steambath of getting one, would you? You'd be a different person, living somewhere else entirely."

At that moment an old car patched together of unmatched parts passes us and honks. I think back over the island cars: mainly old rusty broken-down heaps, except for one antique black Cadillac that leads off the Fourth of July parade, owned by an octogenarian widow from Massachusetts who has to ship it to the island every summer. As we cross over to the beach I see that once again Margaret has brought me back from the hypothetical elsewhere to the here and now. Which is just where I want to be.

A letter arrives from a pair of friends in Bali, another magical island. Tim and Hedy are part of an international network of young people who work their way around the world taking odd jobs, from light trucking in London to cocktail hostessing in Tokyo to teaching, translating, dubbing, anything. Newly married, Tim has taken a leave of absence from his college teaching post to join this network; for the past month, he and Hedy have been in Bali.

In their first letter, they'd had only praise for the lush tropical island and its inhabitants, gentle, artistic, religious. But by their second letter Tim, a scrupulous leftist whose political purity threatens to spoil his year, sounded reluctant and troubled. In this one, despite Hedy's obvious pleasure, he openly agonizes. How can Bali possibly be as delightful as it seems, he worries, with Indonesia in the hands of a reactionary government? Every time he feels caught up in the island's pleasures and beauties he pulls back, searching for flaws.

" 'Yesterday we had the good luck to attend a temple wedding,' " I read aloud. " 'We were very excited when Hedy's dance teacher invited us. Religion is the center of

Balinese life—everywhere, you see offerings of fresh flowers and fruits at the hundreds of temples and shrines. But once we arrived at the wedding, I began to feel uncomfortable. The ceremony was fascinating, with gamelan music and amazing dances, but the hidden misery of these subject people made it impossible for me to enjoy the wedding after the first ten minutes.' "

Margaret shakes her head. "Oh, for Pete's sake! Can you imagine choosing to dwell on misery with the gamelan playing and everyone dancing? 'Hidden' misery at that?"

"I wonder what Hedy thinks," I say, putting down the letter. "If only Tim's politics were less—"

"Politics, pooh," says Margaret. "Does he once report seeing suffering or oppression? Is he genuinely moved or just mouthing what he's heard? That's not politics, that's pride. He needs to think of himself as a certain sort of man regardless of what he really sees or feels." Then she tells the story of one of her sons who was so hooked on thinking of himself as a runner that for a long time after a serious leg injury he claimed he would rather be dead than give up running. "It was losing his image of himself as a man, the feeling he got from running, that made him miserable. The rest of his life was okay—he had friends, a good job, the pain was under control, he was even able to swim every day. But his self-image had become so out of phase with reality that he wanted to shoot his own leg. Just like Tim."

Or me? I wonder, thinking of the seaweed in my New York cupboard.

" 'The fault-finder will find faults even in paradise.' That's Thoreau," says Margaret.

I search her face, extremely curious to hear what more she thinks about this issue, since I'm often disturbed by the politics of my own pleasures. "Sometimes," I confess, "I wonder what I'm doing here, filling my days with all this joy when there's so much suffering in the world. Sometimes I feel guilty to be so . . . lucky."

Margaret shrugs dismissively. "Do you really think the world would be better off if you were suffering too? Adding your tears to the pot?"

I ponder this. True, I may not be doing harm off here by myself, but for an activist used to hell-raising, does that count?

"Depends who's counting," says Margaret, shading her eyes. "To me, it looks like you're doing okay. You're caring for this place, you're getting clear about things, you're writing. And the more consciousness in the world, the better off it is."

"Everything you mention brings me pleasure. It's for me, not the world."

"That's how consciousness usually works," she says wryly.

"But how can that be enough?"

She leans back till her eyes are in the roof's shade but the rest of her is in the sun. "Enough? Who said anything about enough?"

NO one would ever guess what spectacular feasts we mount every day. Sitting down to another exquisite meal, we chuckle, recalling that back in the city our friends feel sorry for us up here all alone, living "without the amenities." One of Margaret's daughters begged her to phone her daily to reassure her that she was still alive, and that very week my Parisienne friend Hélène wrote teasingly, "Confess, aren't you longing by now for a boeuf en daube or a galantine de volaille?" We laugh as we stuff ourselves with bouillabaisse.

Long a master at making do, Margaret teaches me as much about food as I teach her. She shows me how to flavor with lemon peel, spike teas with spices, combine grains and legumes to fortify protein, make brownies from cocoa, grate tubers into pancake batter. And one night, as we groan from overeating, she offers to teach me the pleasures of a fast.

I'm excited but skeptical, afraid I'll fail. "What will it do to us?"

"Clean out the poisons, charge your energies. Often, fasting makes things clear. If you don't like it, you can always eat."

But I do like it, like the sense of my body it induces, the new awareness. For the next thirty-six hours we take nothing but water and tea, getting higher and higher. My perceptions grow keener, our jokes funnier. Too alert to sleep, I fill my notebook with sketches of the nubble under the quarter moon while Margaret naps. At the first light, I wake her for the sunrise, and we head for Dedgers where, perched on even the highest rock, we're drenched with numinous spray.

WE'RE outside, breakfasting on freshly baked muffins—half of them laced with dock seeds, half with newly ripened elderberries. A stiff breeze riffles the brush. Margaret looks up at the sky and announces she'll be leaving soon.

"Soon? When?"

"It's up in the air—depends on the weather. Possibly tomorrow."

"Tomorrow! Then we'd better celebrate tonight," I say.

I have no sense of how long she's been here; in nubble time, things that happened yesterday often feel like weeks ago, and vice versa. I'm both relieved and sorry to see her go: relieved to resume my experiment in solitude, but sorry to lose the company of the one person I know whose sympathy for my chosen life is incontestable, though she'd never choose it for herself.

An hour later, clothed from neck to toe, we're behind the cabin, waist-high in brambles, picking raspberries. After last night's rain they glisten like garnets. Their flavor puts to shame the bland sameness of store-bought ones. We move slowly through the brush, stretching and balancing like Tai Chi masters, exploring each curve and corner, learning the intimate secrets of each patch as we reach and bend, caressing the canes, nosing out the secret places. Ripe berries fall into our hands at the first touch, those that resist we leave to ripen, the overripe we eat on the spot.

When my bowl is full I look around for Margaret, but she's strayed out of sight. Retracing my path to the cabin, I see how many berries I've missed. They'll keep flowering and ripening till mid-October, so I leave them for the birds. Down on the beach I hail a lobsterman pulling his traps in Shark Cove and buy two large one-clawed lobsters ("culls") he's glad to dispose of, which I store beneath the cabin in a basket lined with rockweed for insulation.

It's a sun-drenched late-summer evening as we set the table on the front deck for our farewell lobster banquet. The bathers are gone; only a few herring gulls and a couple of sea crows call past one another on the wide beach. While the lobsters steam in three inches of boiling seawater, we eat our starters. Fresh sea-urchin roe, so prized in Japan; my dandelion-bud popcorn; sorrel soup, or *schav*, made from the weed that surrounds the cabin. Twenty minutes later, as we put down our spoons, the lobsters are done.

Like most people, Margaret has never had lobster fresh from the sea. I teach her the art of finding every last morsel of meat—not just the large chunks from tail and claw that people dare in restaurants, but the bits of muscle in the legs and flippers, the sweet morsels separated by cartilage hiding behind the lungs, the red roe, and the rich green tomalley, or liver, that fills the body cavity.

As we crack the claws and suck the legs, for the last time we discuss my divorce. A pacifist, Margaret tells me how it's the war itself, not the outcome, that threatens to undo me, how negative thoughts—rage, regret, envy, anxiety—are powerful poisons that corrode the guts of their possessors quite as much as those of their intended victims.

I hear what she says. I even recognize that rage and fear are already stealing my sleep, harming my children. But I don't see how, if Jerry wants a fight, I can avoid one. "You don't know Jerry," I say. "He's a demon fighter, he'll bring out all the heavy weapons. That's one of the reasons I could never bring myself to leave him—I was too terrified to start a war. You should have seen him with his first wife. Believe me, I know this man."

Margaret shrugs. "Okay, if Jerry loves to fight, let *him* do the fighting. He'll hurt himself, not you. And the outcome won't change—you're going to wind up dividing your property roughly in half in any case."

"But what if he gets the nubble?"

"He can't unless you agree."

She knows a lot, but she doesn't know Jerry. I suddenly recall the man in an auto shop who came at him with a crowbar, threatening to kill him if he didn't leave at once. To Jerry the episode demonstrated his own self-restraint, since (lacking a weapon) he'd refused to fight back. But to me it was just one more confirmation of his aggression—great enough to provoke someone to threaten him with a crowbar. "But what if he does?" I ask, growing agitated.

"Then you'll find somewhere else to live. Which will be fine, because whatever's happening here is probably happening everywhere."

This is the kind of blanket statement I often find irritating, but I don't want to be sidetracked by an argument.

"Everything you've learned here," Margaret continues, "will go with you. And what you haven't yet learned you'll be able to discover somewhere else. That's what it means to be on your path—your understanding will just keep deepening."

"*Po*," I answer, wishing I could believe her, but afraid.

"Don't you see? It isn't the place. It's you. Otherwise, you wouldn't have come to the nubble all those years without a clue to what was possible. And now that you know, you'll know it anywhere."

"Anywhere except Cleveland," I add, only half joking.

"Even Cleveland," she insists. Before I can object, she offers me the cryptic words of Buddha: *You cannot travel on the path before you have become the path itself.* "That means even if it leads you right smack through the center of Cleveland."

As I cut the tart packed with fresh-picked berries, it does seem a waste to focus on remote hypothetical events when at this moment, with the gulls assembling for their twilight concert on Obed's Rock and the armada of ducks massing behind the Shmoos, this delectable feast is still going on.

WHEN the moon, orange as an egg yolk, appears over the outhouse, we go down to the beach for a last walk together. Sometimes by flashlight we've followed crabs marching boldly across the sand, but tonight as I toss the lobster shells back to the ocean Margaret notices a strange glimmer in the water. Tiny phosphorescent organisms shimmer on the crest of each wave like a neon sketch, only to break up and scatter on the wet sand. We try to scoop up the sparkling creatures in our hands and hold them long enough to examine them by flashlight, but in the bright beam their own light disappears.

As we start back to the cabin, the moon, which we last saw rising over the outhouse, has paled from orange to lemon and rolled clear over the nubble to South Beach, where it's about to set. We're mystified—how could it travel so far so fast? While we speculate, something bounds down the stairs from the deck and streaks past us across the beach toward the woods. We grab each other's hands and freeze, holding our breath, till it disappears behind the dunes. From its wild beauty loping across the sand I know it's a fox, though I've never seen one except in zoos. What was it doing on the deck? How did it get there? To me it's like Margaret herself, streaking momentously through my life.

I see the fox again that night in a long complicated dream in which a fox, a seal, and a heron live together with me in a seaweed forest on the ocean floor, all perfectly at home in that liquid medium. When I wake early to the dawn chorus, I turn my face into my pillow, hoping to prolong the dream. The next time I wake, the sun is high, and a lobster boat is chugging through the cove. I go to Margaret's room to tell her my dream, but her bed, neatly made, is empty and her things are gone. She must have caught the early boat. Weighted to her pillow with a Bathtub rock is a farewell note, written in her curly script, containing her hostess gift: "The next time you're in town please take $25.00 from your bank account and use it to buy something you fancy but wouldn't think of buying for yourself, and consider it a gift from me." Above her familiar signature the note ends cryptically, "Remember the fox."

Not till six weeks later, when the days have grown short and the nights chilly, do I finally manage to get to Portland.

After I've finished all my chores, I stroll through the Old Port shops, searching for Margaret's gift. Back when the children were little and usually barefoot, I banned from the cabin anything glass or fragile, except for an occasional found object. Now I overturn my rule. In the Asian shop I select a teapot to replace the battered aluminum coffeepot with which I've always made do. Elegantly shaped, it is decorated in a traditional Chinese blue-and-white pattern, with a delicate rice-grain design in the transluscent porcelain. I pay by check and ask the clerk to wrap it as a gift.

EIGHT

BACK in the city. The crises resume. Meat again; waste; consumption; conflict; politics. Living with the Wall, a door away from a man who has sworn himself my enemy, does nothing to enhance my work; indeed, far lesser threats can kill the concentration I need to write. Jerry and I communicate by telephone or by passing notes under a closed door; still, I wonder if he doesn't tap my phone, read my mail, and enter my locked files when I go out, keeping a log on me for his lawyer. The Wall we hoped would insure our independence seems to be having an opposite effect. With Watchbirds hovering everywhere, my confidence falters, my work loses momentum. I slash at my manuscript with black Magic Marker until it begins to resemble censored government files as whole episodes unwrite themselves.

Then the inevitable happens. One cloudy winter morning I look up from my computer to see Jerry's heavy body filling the doorway between our living quarters. Glowering ferociously, he waves a paper and begins to shout, and suddenly all the noisy fights we've ever had come tumbling into the living room. When the children lived with us I tried to remove our quarrels to a café around the block or postpone them till the children were asleep. But now that we're alone there's nothing to temper our fury.

When I stand and protest the intrusion, defiantly Jerry folds his arms across his chest, sets his head at a cocky angle, and challenges me to close the door. A terrible argument ensues. All the decorum we've observed over the months since my return to the city breaks down. He takes a heavy step toward me, into my space, raises his voice, his hand —and suddenly I too am raging. Though we were yoked together for decades, I feel as threatened as if he were the hacker. Icily I ask him to leave. "Make me!" he answers. We accuse and indict until we're shouting in each other's faces. When he finally withdraws over the threshold, I cross the room to close the door. He pulls it open again. Soon we are tugging at the door from opposite sides like ten-year-olds. Ugly passion spills over the doorjamb.

So much for civilized divorce. So much for best intentions.

But neither of us dares move out and relinquish our major asset. Acknowledging our equal claims to it, we close the door and try again.

MARGARET once told me that the Chinese word for *crisis* contains the character for *opportunity*. Just as my family crisis reaches its zenith, I receive a long-distance call from one Professor Nadine Kandel, sweet-voiced deus ex machina who heads a University of Colorado writing program, inviting me to spend a year as Visiting Writer-in-Residence. I'm stunned. Colorado is a name and shape I last considered in fourth grade, memorizing its location on a blank map along with those of half a dozen other Western states from which I can now only vaguely distinguish it.

I learned quite young that opportunities are a matter of luck; it took me longer to understand that acting upon them is always up to you. Hasn't Margaret promised me I can now live anywhere without losing what I've learned? Now's my chance to see. Not to mention the relief of getting away from Jerry.

The offer comes on a Friday. For form's sake I ask for the weekend to think it over, but I already know my answer. When I call her back on Monday Professor Kandel offers to help me find a place to live. I describe my housing needs: quiet, furnished, affordable, with a guest room if possible for Margaret and the children, preferably non-suburban.

"How would you feel about living in the mountains? The university owns some cottages up in the Flatirons that may be available."

Mountains? Flatirons? I know nothing about mountains. Crossing by train through the Alps and the mysterious Pyrenees decades before, their immense alien peaks piercing the sky, I'd felt them vaguely threatening. But having recently expanded my landlocked life to embrace the ocean, where a whole new world awaited me, I'm ready to take on mountains too. "Why not?" I reply.

Jerry is so tickled at the prospect of getting rid of me that he offers me his car, an old Chevy which he no longer needs now that he's back in the city. He arranges for his nephew, who is going to the West Coast, to drive the car to Boulder and hitchhike on from there. I move my files to mini-storage, pack my computer and clothes into the car trunk, buy a plane ticket with open return, and with a minimum of baggage sally west.

A cat is waiting on the doorstep of the small cottage that Nadine Kandel found for me seven thousand feet above sea level. Not just any cat, but one that looks like our old black-and-white cat Kiwi, who died three years ago. He rubs against my legs and purrs as if he's been expecting me.

Bending down to stroke him, I'm startled by the similarities to Kiwi: same markings, mad leaps, insistent whine, even the same intolerance of having his tail touched. And when he's invariably waiting to greet me when I return from school, pushing right into the house with a loud cry and staying until dinnertime, I have to invoke Margaret's useful *po* over whether or not this cat is Kiwi reincarnate. After all, I'm in Boulder now, regional capital of the New Age, where in the thin mountain air people search out their past lives as avidly as others research their family trees.

The small, modestly furnished cottage is the first house I've ever rented by myself. I love it at once—love the old yellow Depression dishes, the oak lamps, the sun streaming into my bedroom window casting on the window shade silhouettes of leaves resembling Japanese calligraphy. It was built in the nineteenth century as part of a historic Chautauqua community—one of more than a hundred such colonies throughout the United States, each clustered around an auditorium where, long before radio or television, orators, artists, and politicians built their reputations on the Chautauqua circuit. Now owned by the University of Colorado, this Chautauqua, one of the few still standing, connects me to the historic past. Emma Goldman, Houdini, Clarence Darrow, Susan B. Anthony herself may all have performed here, perhaps slept in my very cottage in the shadow of the looming mountains.

On my daily mail run to the Chautauqua office I feel the mountains over my shoulder stalking me. Unpredictable as the ocean, they change form without warning, from jagged to craggy to smooth to fluid, like living things, sometimes shrouded in darkness, sometimes glowing in light, sometimes haloed in purple haze, sometimes dewy, silver, electric, or burnished, reflecting the autumn gold of the shimmering aspens. Sitting at my computer on the glassed-in sun porch, my back to the windows on which the mountains cast their shadows, I wonder how I've managed to live half a century without getting to know one.

Everyone I meet, faculty, staff, and students, seems so comfortable with the mountains that hiking, biking, climbing, skiing, even leaping off a peak with a parachute are normal parts of their daily lives, as I discover in my students' stories. Every weekend they pile their equipment into their cars, their pickups, their four-wheel-drives and take off for some state forest.

Though I drive to work every day, I myself am a reluctant driver, having had the rare good fortune to spend my adult life on two islands where a car is both unnecessary and undesirable; here, with a trailhead just steps from my door, I can begin my hikes from home instead of navigating hairpin turns on treacherous mountain roads. To prepare myself for the formidable wooded trails, I buy a pair of sturdy hiking boots and stretch my muscles near my house in the steep treeless meadow covered with strange feathery grasses and small cacti. Each day after my morning class I return to the meadow, following the path toward the heights. Its steepness often leaves me winded, but I press on, climbing higher every day, feeling a pull in my calves and a flush of achievement even though I always stop short of the forest. At the meadow's edge I find a ring of small trees covered with tart wild plums. I fill my hat and cook up marvelous jams and pastries, returning frequently for more. Then one late-September day, seeing that the birds and animals have finally finished off the crop, I leave the familiar meadow to ascend into the rugged unknown.

THE forest: by reputation treacherous or magical, depending on your attitude, like the forests in fairy tales. Recall the notorious wooded ravine of your childhood, where children were said to have been abducted and everyone, boys and girls alike, was strictly forbidden to play. Unlike Red Ridinghood, Snow-White, Hansel and Gretel taking their chances in the woods, I've been drilled in the dangers: Will I take a wrong turn among the white spruce, the mountain hemlock, the Douglas fir and be trapped in the woods after dark? Will the mountain lion smell me out? Or the hacker (who here is transformed to a woodsman)? But once I'm on the path, all the fears threatening to resurface dissolve in the sensual surprise, the scents, the green pleasure of these woods. The path is marked, the rise gradual, the sunlight bright and playful filtering through the leaves. Though the rarefied air of these altitudes notoriously tires out newcomers, leaving them giddy, sick, or short of breath, and though I am hardly in shape for a strenuous climb, instead of tiring, I feel my spirit and strength expanding with each switchback, each new breath of mountain air. My thoughts lengthen; I pick up energy; my nubble senses take over, making everything here feel new, or old in a new way: the pungent odors, the springy carpet of decaying leaves on the forest floor, the sonorous knock and creak of the branches overhead, the flickering light and shade, the unfamiliar lichens, fungi, and wildflowers, the curious insects, lizards, rodents, birds that slither and dart around me as if I were invisible, the silence itself, so different from the silence at the shore where the constant surge of surf and cry of gulls lie just below consciousness.

This aging body, soon to be old, surprises me. Out on the trails I find it serviceable, sturdy, reliable. The sleek muscled bodies of the young who occasionally sprint past me or pedal their bikes up the mountain paths are no better designed than mine, though they will doubtless outlast me. The higher I climb, the more I appreciate my body's balance, sensory apparatus, capacity to feel and think, its stamina, strength, integrity—in short, its human perfection. Gone now along with vanity the miserable parade of defects it constantly sprang on me in my youth. (Maybe this is what George Sand meant when she wrote, "The day I buried my youth I grew twenty years younger.") Muscled only by the vicissitudes of my haphazard experience and potluck of genes, it gets me where I want to go with ease and, after a week of exhilarating climbs, even a modicum of grace.

On Saturday I phone my city children to entice them out for Thanksgiving, dangling before them mountain marvels and prepaid tickets.

SOON , like many locals, I forgo the traditional o.j. to begin my day by cleansing my liver with a thimbleful of freshly squeezed wheat-grass juice, then sweeping the health-food stores. Though it reminds me a bit of orach, my passion for wild food has cooled, now that the wild plums are gone. Not that my interest in local gastronomy has slackened, but in Boulder, years ahead of the East Coast in ecological awareness, the surprise is health food, not wild food. At the lavish Alfalfa's market no fewer than fifty different kinds of grains and legumes, mostly organic, are displayed in row after row of shiny bins. Here are cheeses made without animal-based rennet, countless tofu products, hormone-free beef from pampered steers, and an astounding variety of lush produce, including many species new to me, artistically piled in huge colorful mounds. The sheer range of "organic" and "natural" foods, of freshly ground nut butters, fruit nectars, and honeys collected from a variety of flowers, stretches my consciousness, as wild food did before. On my bedside table my copy of *Edible Native Plants of the Rocky*

Mountains lies unread (like the unused bag of seaweed in New York), replaced by a mounting pile of Alfalfa's weekly newsletters covering the virtues of whole grains, the dangers of hormones, holistic health tips, recipes, and warnings about the mounting contamination of the food supply.

THE hacker, whom I managed to ward off on the island and elude in the mountain woods, assumes the form of a breather—one of the liabilities of having a phone. Disturbing my weekend solitude, he usually calls around midnight, breathing heavily, ignoring my increasingly exasperated hellos that climax in my hanging up, then waits until I'm back asleep to call again, forcing me to disconnect the phone and risk missing the possible emergency call from my children, for whose sake I've had the thing installed.

After several weekends of midnights, he calls one Friday at the hour most working people are just getting home. I'm stirring a potful of soup and listening to the news when the phone rings. This time when I answer, instead of merely breathing, my nemesis plunges into conversation, assaulting me with the blunt question: "Do you like to be eaten out?"

"*What*?"—mistrusting my ears.

"Do you like to be eaten out?" he repeats in his deep rough voice.

Shocked by the weird question I hang up, but I immediately regret my automatic response. Since he opened the channels by speaking, shouldn't I have taken him on? Stirring the pot, I imagine all sorts of savvy replies I might have made, from shaming him to telling him off to calling his bluff. Yes, I decide, the thing to do with a control freak like a breather is to call his perverted bluff.

When the phone rings again a moment later, giving me

a second chance, I'm ready. To the same rude question I confront him with, "Yes, actually, I do," and throw out the insolent challenge, "You offering?"

As I expected, he's unprepared for this assault. After a long puzzled pause he retreats to: "Do you like to be fingered?"

"Not particularly."

Another silence while I stir my soup. Then he ventures again: "What else do you like to do?"

"What do you suggest?" I shoot back, hoping my aggressive questions will rattle him as he intends his to humiliate me. I tap my fingers impatiently against the phone. "Well?" I prompt, confident I'm safe since my address is unlisted. Evidently he has reached the limit of his imagination, for at this point he reverts from words to breathing.

I press my advantage: "Nothing else, really; that's quite enough for me."

Too much, however, for him. He hangs up.

The next day when he calls back at the same hour to repeat his questions, I'm ready for him. To throw a scare into his fantasies I cover the phone and yell at my imaginary kids to quiet down, can't they see I'm on the phone? Then, speaking into the receiver, I say, "Look, I know you're not really serious about this, so stop wasting my time," and hang up.

And he never calls back.

WEEKDAYS I teach fiction workshops for undergraduates, throwing myself into the work as never before, in gratitude for this challenging godsend of a job. Ever since my first book was published I've had adjunct teaching posts around New York, temporary part-time fiction workshops at low pay with no benefits or security, which as a feminist I nevertheless welcomed as opportunities to pass on what I know and learn from the young. This job is different. It's full time and well paid—what my brother, who doesn't understand the difficulty of a writing life, calls "a *real* job." My students, who may write whatever they like for me, astound me with their stories, written or whispered. During office hours they tug me into their worlds as sheepishly, shyly, desperately they close my office door to drop their book bags on the floor and lay their confusions and panic on my green steel desk: in the first month alone three distraught women and one young man seek comfort (and deadline extensions) over unwanted pregnancies and secret abortions. They write stories about their treacherous bodies, their families who don't understand, childhood humiliations, athletic triumphs, the cruelties of love. Shy and manic alike submit their fragile egos to public scrutiny as we work our way around the conference table with our "constructive critiques." This semester they imitate Faulkner, reject Beckett, revere Rich. I note down their responses in a little red notebook, praise them, lend them books. I try to teach them what I know, all the while uncertain if writing can be taught. Grading them is painful, but I do it. Some rage, some weep, some claim to suffer writer's block. Some stay after class and follow me devotedly around the campus. One belligerent junior who always arrives in class late and never reads the assignments turns violent, throwing his books against the wall, then drops out. (What have I done?) The night before each class I scrutinize their stories and prepare my comments; the rest of the time I reserve for my own writing.

At first I'm overwhelmed by everything New Age, though it is exhilarating to discover an entire community claiming to live by the same principles I uncovered in the solitude of the nubble. Is this what Margaret meant by claiming that what can be found anywhere can probably be found everywhere? But gradually my excitement turns to puzzlement. If I expected to find in the famously spiritual ambiance of Boulder a pace and atmosphere more in keeping with the nubble's than with New York's, I am brought up short by how much money changes hands in its name. It's not only that every spiritual group and mystical cult in the country has an outreach office in Boulder, or that the radio's round-the-clock transcendental space music and Sunday-morning New Age sermons are interrupted by frequent advertisements for meditation classes and infant massage, but entire incense-scented bookstores are devoted to the occult, grandiose health-food emporiums outshine even the largest supermarkets, and psychics and clairvoyants line the pedestrian mall. The movement born as an alternative to the arid materialism of consumer culture is here hawked and promoted like any commercial venture.

Perhaps I was naïve to hope for the purity of solitude in the middle of a city—any city, even a purportedly visionary one like Boulder—the essence of which is commerce and exchange. But remembering my foolish friend in Bali whose critical stance kept him needlessly glum and aloof, I vow to hold myself open to the valuable kernel that lies at the heart of each human production—like the indisputably lovable core buried in each human soul—hoping to sustain, perhaps even expand, the knowledge I gained at the nubble.

Most of my teaching colleagues, I'm shocked to learn, consider the university a besieged island of hard-nosed reason floating in a muddy sea of New Age philistinism. They're suspicious of all modes of awareness other than the rational-scientific. Though I long shared their bias, now I am distressed to hear them snidely lambaste the Buddhists for "taking over the town." They dismiss the distinguished faculty of the Naropa Institute as "frivolous," even challenging their integrity. "The Buddhists are so manipulative, they wear business suits in order to ingratiate themselves with the community," confides an associate professor of English in hushed tones; and when I protest, the professor cautions, "Wait till you've been here awhile, you'll see." In fact, what I come to see is quite the opposite. As I study Buddhist texts to know what I'm defending, I keep on finding the spirit of the nubble.

At a party in honor of new faculty I meet a young anthropologist from Stanford named Clara Lavin. The way she deliberates before speaking, cocks her pretty head to one side like an alert bird, and furrows her brow reflectively in conversation makes me think of Amy, though they look nothing alike. Since Clara also lives in Chautauqua, I offer her a lift home. On that brief ride up the mountain we discover unexpected affinities: both newcomers, both feminist activists, both struggling with manuscripts, both curious about the local culture. Despite the twenty-year gap in our ages (or perhaps because of it: she wants to see what's coming, I want to know what's new) we begin riding together. To and from school, on mundane errands, and finally for the pleasure of exploring. Although she keeps an old VW parked outside her cottage, Clara prefers to ride with me, having lost her nerve for driving after a scary accident. It surprises me that I, least confident of drivers, should willingly assume the role of chauffeur—but then, every new undertaking seems surprising.

Clara, with her anthropological imagination, is as eager as I to search out the substance beneath Boulder's flashy New Age veneer. From our first field trip to one of the biweekly Hare Krishna open-house dinners I recognize her as an ideal partner despite her shyness—serious, curious, learned. Alone, I would be too embarrassed to respond to those chanting, dancing, tambourine-shaking youths with their shining faces, saffron-colored robes, and shaven heads who stand on the pedestrian mall every weekend handing out free cookbooks (*Higher Taste: A Guide to Gourmet Vegetarian Cooking and a Karma-Free Diet*); but beside Clara I'm willing to brave it. When Saturday evening comes, we park down the block from the Krishna house and approach on foot in order to peek through the windows and see what we're getting ourselves into. The interior, though unfurnished, is handsome and spotless, with baseboards, mantels, and banisters of gleaming oak and several leaded Art Nouveau-style stained-glass windows typical of turn-of-the-century Colorado houses. A large Krishna doll, colorfully clothed, is seated on a shrine in the middle of the living room; from the open door aromas of spices and incense beckon to us. "You go first," says Clara, hanging back from the door. "No, you," I counter. Disguising our skepticism with smiles, finally we enter together.

Someone hands us each a paper plate loaded with appetizing food: crisp fried dumplings, curried soup, thin noodles topped with a subtle mixture of spiced vegetables, and a delicate sweet custard. We join several dozen others seated on the floor, quietly eating. From the first taste I know it's holy food.

After the meal, while we sip aromatic tea, a tall bald Caucasian man, older than the others though younger than I, comes slowly down the stairs in his bare feet, playing a sweet melodious song on a wooden flute to the accompaniment of tambourines, bells, and drum. When he's finished, he bows to the guests, with palms and fingers pressed together, and performs certain slow rituals; then he offers a brief introduction to Krishna consciousness.

As he talks, I think back to the first feminist organizing teas we held in meeting halls and church basements back in the late Sixties, when New York was a seething hotbed of rebellion. We served strong coffee, brownies, and gooey pastries—stimulating fare for women about to spring out of their repressive roles like dancing girls leaping from a pasteboard cake. Instead of music we offered honest talk and a whiff of freedom. Now, fifteen years and half a continent later, I'm listening to the soft-spoken pitch of the gentle followers of Krishna promising a life of music, dancing, chanting, happiness itself in exchange for renouncing meat and materialism. Surely, says Clara afterward, there's more to it. What about suffering and oppression? I agree, but I can't help thinking how some outsiders misunderstood our feminist message too, mistakenly thinking it simple.

After that initiation, it's easier for us to pursue our investigations in a spirit of *po*. We sample a ritual bath, soaking ourselves in a rented hot tub till our skin puckers, then open our pores in the sauna to sweat out the poisons, and close them again in the icy waters of a cold plunge, following a local custom that Clara traces back to ancient Rome. Whatever its origin, it's so invigorating that we regularly return, and once we drive all the way up to a Buddhist monastery in the mountains to bathe by starlight in a hot tub, surrounded by stone gardens and sacred pines, open to the sky.

At Rajneesh House we watch videos of the beautiful Indian master with the flowing silver beard and pooling eyes, Margaret's sometime guru Bhagwan Shree Rajneesh, who tells parables in a dreamy voice to a roomful of disciples all dressed in shades of red, with the master's picture on a ribbon around their necks. We chant at a Shinto shrine. We attend two trances: one by a popular Native American psychic guide who executes extraordinary contortions of the body as well as of the vocal cords, another by a trans-channeler recommended by a graduate student of Clara's. This psychic, named Loretta, is a skinny woman of forty-five with a deep Southern voice who assumes in her trance the unlikely form of a short fat twelve-year-old Bengali boy named something like Rufus, whose high nasal voice describes in strangely accented English half a dozen past lives of each of the ten novices in the room. Clara is impressed by Rufus's access to details of her personal history. "There's no way he could have learned that in advance," she insists. But I, content to count my past lives those I've led since emerging from my mother's womb, am impressed less by Rufus than by Loretta, who, before going under, described fear as negative faith, explaining that what you fear you will invariably draw to yourself. Of course! I whispered to Clara, thinking of failure, dogs, loneliness.

Susan G., who's been sent my name by a New York friend, phones to welcome me to Boulder. A longtime Buddhist (though born a Methodist and raised a Catholic) who earns a modest living teaching journal writing at Naropa and giving private Tarot readings, she seems conversant with every esoteric strand of Boulder's eclectic soul. At first I take her for a dilettante; but as I get to know her I recognize the seriousness of her aspirations to increase her psychic powers. Believing (like Margaret) that all spiritual paths converge, she sees no contradiction among the many varied approaches to her professional development. Most recently, Susan's interest in Tarot has led her to the Kabbalah, a branch of Jewish mysticism she pursues weekly in a small study group led by a renowned Denver rabbi. When she invites me to be her guest one cold Monday night, I accept gratefully, despite an aversion to rabbis dating back to my rebellious Sunday-school days.

Dark and intense, with wiry black hair growing out of his nostrils and ears, up his neck, and covering his hands and head, this rabbi looks more like some medieval demon than a holy man. But after he presents the day's paradoxical text from the Apocrypha ("Set not thy heart upon thy goods; and say not, I have enough for my life"), explicating it in his soothing voice as he fixes us with his eyes, I feel my mind stretch and vibrate as it did on the nubble.

WHEN rumors begin to circulate that the CIA is planning a recruiting campaign on campus, this veteran activist joins the group organizing a resistance. From the first meeting I see that even protest politics have a distinctive Boulder slant. In contrast to the noisy confrontational activists from whom I learned my militant political style on the streets of New York, Boulder's left-wing activists are chasteningly soft-spoken. Meetings begin with hand-holding, people sit cross-legged on the floor, discussions are low-keyed, decisions are by consensus, talk is of conscience, reconciliation, love. In place of the familiarly intense, disheveled, secular or Jewish intellectuals who, index fingers raised, so rousingly led the anti-war movement back East, here lean Quakers raise their arms in quiet exhortation, while Buddhists breathe deeply in the lotus position resting their hands, palms up, on their knees. In my experience, activist and spiritual lives are separate realms, the one based in human society, the other in solitude and nature. But here they sit together in a circle, holding hands.

On the day the CIA recruiters arrive on campus, chanting demonstrators guard the entrances, and a festive crowd of supporters spreads across the lawn at the main entrance. Under a bright morning sun, those of us on the wrong side of the barricades wait in orderly lines, single file, to be arrested. The atmosphere is calm; even the police seem touched by the Boulder spirit. In New York back in the Sixties, helmeted police ruthlessly rode their neighing horses straight into crowds of protesters sitting down in the streets surrounding the induction center; but in Eighties Boulder, the police, who seem more like fellow actors than antagonists, spent the night before this demonstration negotiating with the Peace Consortium to work out a precise procedure for arrests. The whole scene seems strangely ceremonial, like a pageant, from our plan to make citizens' arrests of CIA recruiters down to a typed script of questions and responses for police and protesters to follow.

Every so often someone on our side raises a megaphone to announce the number of arrests so far, and a cheer goes up, bringing a few more people over from the spectator side to ours. By afternoon there are so many of us waiting our turn that the police start taking us two, then three, at a time. When it's finally my turn, I link arms with two students, one scrubbed, one grungy, and together we walk to meet our arresting officers, who order us to halt and hand us the script. Will we leave peacefully of our own accord? No. Do we intend to commit civil disobedience? Yes. Once, twice, three times they order us, in the name of the law, to step back from a certain imaginary line our shoes have crossed. We refuse. Then, invoking the powers of the state, they announce our arrest and hand us over to two more officers who, without touching us, politely usher us to the old-fashioned school buses serving as paddy wagons, while the crowd cheers.

At first I distrust this seeming complicity with the police. Isn't this what we've learned to call *co-optation*? But when two days and nearly five hundred arrests later the CIA departs without having held a single interview, I begin to appreciate Boulder's gentle style of protest. Given the hostile political environment—Colorado, after all, will eventually become the first state to pass an anti-gay referendum—this style is no small achievement. And when a month later the district attorney drops all charges against us on the deliciously ironic grounds that he prefers to keep us from "manipulating the criminal justice system" for our "anti-government propaganda campaign," my appreciation solidifies into respect.

The Boulder style is at its best at the Rocky Flats nuclear weapons plant, seven miles south of town, where a prayer vigil is held every Sunday. Sometimes doctors and nurses assemble to minister to a languishing Mother Earth (head an inflated globe, body a long rag doll), poisoned by emissions of plutonium over three decades of burn-offs and accidents; sometimes gardeners cultivate a symbolic garden outside the West Gate to show what could grow in that barren land in place of death; sometimes a dozen show up, sometimes hundreds, but there are always at least a few people singing, praying, and meditating before those gates through which pass radioactive materials for every nuclear weapon in the U.S. arsenal. Chanting among them, I see that politics and spirituality, those seemingly discordant airs, can merge into a single harmonious song whose tune I hope one day to carry on my own.

CLARA, who comes from California, is a seasoned hiker; I am merely an enthusiast. At least once a week we arrange to meet at the top of our road to hike the mountain trails behind Chautauqua at the end of the workday, and often of a weekend we climb into my car and venture onto a higher, more distant mountain. In her backpack Clara carries books to help us identify animal tracks, spores, birds, lichens, wildflowers, and trees, turning our hikes into quests and treasure hunts. One ingenious guide, the *Rocky Mountain Tree Finder*, clarifies connections for me in a new way.

Itself branching like a tree, it works by an artful system of binary choices: "If the needles are bundled together like this . . . go to next page. If they are not bundled together, go to page 22. . . . If you can easily twirl a needle between thumb and finger, go two paragraphs below. If you can't twirl it, because it's flattened, go to page 25"—and so on, till you run out of choices and the tree you're standing before is pictured and named. Clara teaches me such basic woodland skills as how to gauge directions from shadows, how to locate water, how to read the marks on tree trunks, how to slide on scree. In our wanderings we see hares and beavers, deer and elk, moles and porcupines, pheasants, hawks, and quail; we see wide fields full of prairie dogs standing upright on their hind legs beside their burrows, blinking into the sun, front paws folded beneath their chins; and one long Sunday nearing dusk our vague search for the rare bighorn sheep is rewarded when we cross a ledge and suddenly glimpse a ram with magnificent curved horns surrounded by several smaller ewes, their light rumps flashing as they graze.

But the mountains are more than sanctuaries. They are also ordinary, like bread; essential, like books; invigorating, like discipline; stimulating, like solitude. The path behind my cottage up into the Flatirons, the steep rise through the mountain meadow, even the view of the more distant Rockies visible on a fine day from my office, stretching out along the back of the continent like the spines on the back of a Stegosaurus, begin to color my feelings and shape my thoughts until they inhabit my dreams. Not all my study of Boulder's spiritual pursuits yields the light that comes to me in a single hour on a mountain trail. Contemplating the mountains' profile—the peaks and crannies, the surfaces—is like studying an acquaintance who has unexpectedly become a lover. Abandoning *po*, holding nothing back, I become a hiker.

When the snows fall and temperatures drop into the teens, turning the mountains white and the air crisp as new apples, raccoons come down at night to scavenge around Chautauqua, knocking over the garbage cans if I forget to weight the covers with rocks. Whole families of desperate deer can sometimes be seen searching for food at the edge of the meadow practically in the back yards of some of the cottages. The plump yellow squirrels I had often seen scampering through the trees outside my windows—squirrels whose aspen colors, so different from the grays and blacks of their New York cousins, had delighted me when I first arrived—grow visibly leaner and duller as winter progresses, and a lone porcupine, usually so shy, can now sometimes be seen slowly waddling across the Chautauqua road at dusk like a plush ball.

The Chautauqua management, to forestall the water pipes freezing, advises setting our thermostats high and letting taps run throughout the night, as well as keeping vessels filled with reserve supplies of water, just in case. After my adaptation to scarcity on the nubble it's hard for me to waste heating fuel and hear unused water dribble down the drain, especially since my pipes freeze anyway one Friday night despite the precautions. After that, I revert to my nubble discipline, carefully conserving my water reserves until the maintenance crew arrive with blowtorches to thaw the pipes under the cottage.

When they enter the crawl space to get at the boiler, what should they find but a cozy camp complete with dirty sleeping bag, the past several weeks' newspapers, flashlight batteries, empty soup cans, and a few old men's clothes. Evidently, someone has been living beneath my kitchen floor, taking comfort in the heat of my boiler. Though I'm startled, I take the news of the squatter far more calmly than does the management, who sends around a workman to install a padlock on the flimsy door to my crawl space despite my protests. I see no reason to cut the poor soul off from his meager possessions when he's been so unobtrusive a tenant that I haven't even noticed him, and there's no access to the cottage from below. After a couple of days I unlock the padlock and leave it hanging on the hasp for the rest of the winter in case he should return.

I doubt he'll come. But, no longer afraid of the hacker, I never check below to see, preferring to leave him in peace as he has left me.

An exile from Ohio, I always believed I had blessed my children by raising them in the middle of Manhattan. But after discovering the enchantment of elsewhere, I wanted them to know it too and sent them tickets for a visit.

It's Thanksgiving break, the morning of their arrival. I open my eyes to a world clothed in the exquisite lace of hoarfrost. It covers everything from the curlicues on the lampposts to the needles on the fir trees, and though I know it will make driving hazardous, I rejoice for the children's sake.

They come off the plane bundled in parkas and boots, looking more robust than ever, full of news and stories. But as we drive back toward Boulder beneath the snowcapped mountains they fall silent. Awe or alienation? To fill the void I step up my enthusiastic chatter—on the peaks, the local culture, the wild animals we may see—to which they listen without comment. Ascending the broad road curving up to Chautauqua, I try to divine their responses by checking their eyes in the rearview mirror, but their faces are opaque. They don't mention the hoarfrost or the icicles glistening on the gutters; and once inside the cottage, where nothing familiar welcomes them, they look cautiously around like guests. Steve asks for something to eat as politely as a stranger. "Look in the kitchen," I urge. "Make yourselves at home." But they circulate among the small rooms as gingerly as tourists, reluctant to touch the somewhat shabby furnishings. Perhaps it's the sudden change in altitude, I think, seeing Amy drop her backpack on the floor of the tiny guest room and plop down on one of the twin beds.

As soon as they're rested, I take them for a short hike on the Chautauqua trails, though the sun is already low. Recalling the almost physical fear I once felt myself in the mountains' shadow, I've planned a hike for each day of their brief visit, like a vixen teaching her cubs the forest. At first they respond eagerly: in a sunny clearing Amy lies in the pristine snow to make snow angels while Steve sends a barrage of snowballs flying toward a distant tree. In the colorful hats, scarves, and mittens of their recent childhood they seem like playful animals tumbling through the snow under the protective maternal eye. But later, as we trudge across the mountain paths through pure silences broken only by birdsong and the crackle of snow crust, their faces grow solemn, old. What do they think when a gust of wind dumps a snow shower across our path from an overhanging branch or whips luminous flurries around our heads? I watch their faces for signs, hoping that as they breathe in the crisp air of these higher altitudes they too will prize the extra nearness of the sun.

But their visit is too short, the mountains too strange, and they're suspicious of every change in me. "Funny, you never cared about *nature* when we were growing up," says

Steve archly. "Yeah," echoes Amy, "when Daddy wanted to drive to the country to see the leaves you always wanted to stay home and work. Remember?" she challenges, jutting her chin. "Right," affirms Steve, giving Amy a look. "You never even wanted to go to the nubble."

"That's the whole point. We lived in the city. I didn't know."

"You could have known, though. You did grow up in Ohio," he accuses.

"In a suburb," I say weakly.

What a strange conversation—discussing my past blindness when what really disturbs them is my current enthusiasm, my touting the woods like religion, giving over my allegiance to a life that may seem to have no place for them except a small guest room. They scoff at my claim that the local squirrels are in any way different from those of New York. Steve is annoyed and Amy furious at my glib suggestion that their late beloved Kiwi inhabits the body of a stranger cat. The dangers and mysteries of the snowcapped mountains, whose elevations make hearts pump, spirits soar, and cakes fall, are compounded for them for having seduced their mother away from the family, as the Snow Queen stole away little Hans.

Not that they openly reproach me; indeed, they merely shrug when I tell them I've applied to extend my job another year because, with the divorce still dragging on and my new book coming along, I'm afraid to lose momentum by returning to New York. But instead of sharing my delight in Alfalfa's, or in Boulder's spiritual cornucopia, they hold themselves aloof, exchanging patronizing glances, as if I were now a cultural defector who had traded my responsibility to mend my marriage for some tawdry spiritual thrills. I might have explained that after such freedom as this I couldn't again face living behind a Wall, might have described the risks of searching out another Manhattan apartment before reaching a settlement with Jerry. But I will not defend myself. Haven't Jerry and I both vowed to "leave the children out of it"? Seeing their sad, anxious faces, I wonder if perhaps Jerry has been presenting his side after all. Or maybe the children don't realize how long our marriage has been over. Or perhaps (cruel irony!) they think I've fled not my marriage but them.

This prospect torments me. How can I have been so obtuse as to think that by vacating the battlefield I could spare the children the anguish of their parents' breakup? Holding back tears as I watch them board their plane, unable to distinguish cause from effect (their pain insures mine, as mine creates theirs), I'm caught on the ancient wheel of suffering from which not even the solitude of the nubble or the mountaintop offers refuge.

NINE

A LOVER enters my life, a courtly college friend with whom I had a passionate fling thirty-five years ago. Charles ("Chip") Hawkins, whose name has peppered my dream book over the years and whose photo I never abandoned through two marriages, tracks me down in Boulder and begins to court me long-distance with frequent phone calls and occasional weekend visits. Three tantalizing details reach out from our distant past to snag me again: Charles's animated eyes opening so wide in conversation as to ring the pale blue irises with white; his fingers on the table forming jumping tents for emphasis; and a peculiar voiced sigh that escapes his lips about every third kiss. Behind the mature elegance, ruddy skin, capped teeth, and thinning hair my eye detects the tall shy athletic youth with fair skin, crooked smile, and yellow pompadour I secretly loved in a past life. Each night as I wait for his call I feel my strength on trial; what will become of my hard-won solitude?

Once an earnest athlete, Charles now climbs mountains. With the discipline and ardor required to conquer some of the highest peaks on four continents he hopes to scale new summits—with me! A sculptor, painter, and professional art restorer, he specializes in controlling the temperature and humidity of a work's environment: too dry and a priceless piece might crumble, too moist and it may rot—"like love," he whispers in my ear. As one who tries to embrace whatever temperature or humidity is happening by, I'm suspicious of trying to control anything so primal. But Charles knows his business, visiting me with exactly the right frequency to keep my juices flowing without hardening my resistance. A connoisseur of age, he helps our pasts shine through the present like pentimento, the reemergence on a canvas of an older design. Delving the layers—the marriages and divorces, aspirations and achievements, failures and tragedies—we tell our stories in an erstwhile private code to which we each still hold a key. Is it this secret language of memory, merging past and present, that reunites old lovers? Or is it the youth we see behind the masks of age? Or that rarity, a second chance? This time round, unlike the first, we know who we are—which may be what my mother meant when she praised fifty as "old enough to know."

Much more than a common past unites us; it turns out we are kindred spirits. Like me and Margaret, Charles was transformed at fifty. Like us, he knows that less is more. From a tragic fire in which he lost his only son, his house, his faith in the world, he emerged with a vow to strip down to basics, preferring to live alone and as soon as possible retire to some simple "rubble house" in the woods.

We're talking long-distance when he tells me this dream, so amazingly like my own. I gulp my tea. "A *rubble* house? What's that?"

"A plain stone cabin, on a mountainside. Near a stream if I'm lucky. Maybe a ruin I can fix up. I don't need much—just a couple of rooms. A place where I can live and work and think, do some climbing, maybe ski."

Another solitaire!—the only one I know. I tell him about my *nubble* house. Then on and off through the night I think about that ideal love conjured by Rilke in which "two solitudes protect and border and greet each other." After all, what could be better for an enemy of waste than a recycled lover, or for a loner with a book to write than a long-distance one? For a while the conditions are so propitious that by spring break I have a rough draft of my book. In the brief interval between revisions, we agree to celebrate in Santa Fe.

IT'S an unusually blustery March, with nights so cold that we must keep a fire burning in the adobe fireplace in the corner of our room, where I learn to balance three logs in an upright pyramid, New Mexico fashion. Each morning fresh aromatic logs of piñon and juniper appear outside our door, compliments of the management of the small inn where we've holed up to make love. When we manage to emerge from our room it's smack into the shock of a new culture: remnants of old Spain in the centuries-old street names, traces of ancient Pueblo life in the adobe architecture and pepper-based cuisine that brings cleansing tears to our eyes and guts. Rich tamales of cornmeal, spices, and meat steamed in cornhusk wrappings, hot chiles cooked into thick red and green sauces, blue tortillas made of Indian corn, enchiladas layered with fiery chile and melted cheese baked flat in a stack New Mexico style instead of conventionally stuffed and rolled arouse our appetites. Hotter and wetter we grow each night beside our piñon fire as chiles and love excite our tingling lips.

On our last day, a Sunday, spring bursts onto the broad New Mexico mesas in a blaze of sun. In Santa Fe's elegant central plaza a brass band of portly men in old-fashioned uniforms with brass buttons and gold-braided caps plays Spanish dances and marching airs. Like all the young Sunday lovers promenading through the square, we take a final turn across the grass and under the arcades where Native American artisans display their traditional wares, my hand curled like a kitten in his, his elbow pressed lightly into my ribs, his hip against mine, his long legs slowing to match my gait. It's all I can do not to stop right there in front of everyone while the band plays and curl myself into his arms. Defeat or no, I long to go on touching.

Yet, when we stop in a café at the edge of the plaza for a cup of chocolate, we avoid the question of *next.* He's as reticent as I: is it shyness, prudence, or fear? At that moment, temperature and humidity are just right—why tamper? But later, in the airport, reluctantly clicking off to our separate gates, I feel my body wrenched by opposite pulls as we keep turning back to wave again—as if one more wave could forestall the end.

This sudden new attachment that feels as old as my dreams unnerves me. Have I made myself over in solitude only to lose myself to love? In my window seat practically touching the clouds (which are as white as the whites of Charles's eyes, as the sky is as blue as their blue), I wonder if my solitude has failed me, exposing an emptiness I'm trying to fill with Charles. Or has it so richly filled me that it's brimming over into love?

A university contract for another year awaits me in my mailbox. I sign it immediately. Since I'm obliged to relinquish my cottage for the summer to Texas vacationers who pay triple my winter rent, I decide to place my few possessions in (yet another) mini-storage and drive back to

Santa Fe where, now that I can presumably live anywhere, I'll concentrate on finishing my book.

My summer sublet—a small adobe house in the hills at the edge of town—sits on a slope between a dirt road and the acequia, an irrigation stream that waters the trees in the yard, including two olives, two cherries, a mulberry, and a lemon, plus spreading patches of dill, mint, anise. A dense hedge of currants marks the back boundary of the yard, which ends at a bluff, dropping off to a stream bordered by tall eucalyptus and willow trees; a row of gaudy yuccas, which will eventually bear delicious fruit on their tall flower stalks, marks the front boundary. Something edible seems always to be ripening.

Every day I work on my book in a small darkened room off the shaded portal, breaking when the dense heat lifts in the late afternoon; then I set off on foot to explore the dusty roads of the neighborhood. I seldom see another walker, perhaps because the few houses are guarded by bored dogs who bark ferociously at the approach of any stranger. Teeth bared, they strain at their chains and leap at their confining fences and walls while my old fear comes thudding back, forcing me to keep crossing and recrossing the road. Then I remember: You used to be afraid of dogs but you're not anymore. Clara has taught me the canine-pacifying stance of the Meratus of Java: tongue curled, thumbs tucked into loose fists held at the sides, steady pace. I decide to try it and—voilà!—the charm works its magic not only on me but most of the time also on the dogs, who quickly settle down in the dust.

I use the same technique on a family of black-widow spiders I find nesting on the portal beneath the green-flowered glider cushion just outside my bedroom door, curling my tongue as I study them. They're gorgeous in their way, with a bright red spot, like a pair of reddened lips, beneath the rounded black abdomen. I have no desire to kill these beauties; a lover of spiders, on the nubble I let their webs accumulate in all the corners and eaves of the cabin until the place looks haunted. But preferring not to be bitten, I consult my neighbor, a young mother of three named Yvonne, whose advice will presumably be prudent. "You want me to kill them for you? Get me a broom," she offers. When I hesitate, she tells me that unless I sit on them they probably won't bother me. There are other places to sit, I don't need the glider. That night, as I eat my blue enchiladas out on the portal and listen to the coyotes howling in the hills, inciting the town dogs to a frenzy, I speculate on how many lives you can spare if you're not afraid.

After that, I feel free to wander over the dry scrubby hills, so barren when seen from a car but up close aflame with wildflowers—yellow blazing stars and evening primroses; blue larkspur, lupine, and heliotrope; red Indian paintbrush and sweet-scented scarlet penstemon. Hummingbirds suck from their cupped throats. Succulents and cacti, which I'd once lumped together, display their vast variety in distinctive prickles, flowers, fruits, and shapes, from the jointed cholla to fishhook cactus to beavertails. Huge jackrabbits bob through the scrub and foot-long snakes cross the dirt roads. I study a run-over rattler I take to be dead until it suddenly slithers away. From the roadside I gather armfuls of long, dry grasses—grama grass, whose flowering heads curl into delicate rings, Indian rice grass, apache plume—to set around the house in empty jars, filling my days with amazing grains.

I enjoy them for themselves and also for the thought of Charles's wide eyes when he walks into this blooming house. Do I need him? No. Do I long for him? Every time

I stop to ask. "Just remember," he's told me, "whenever you call, I'll come"—like the wishes proffered in fairy tales. I try my best not to call.

On my bedside table I find an intriguing locally published book: *Peace Pilgrim: Her Life and Work in Her Own Words.* The cover pictures a lone silver-haired woman, probably in her seventies, walking toward the reader along a country road, dressed in dark pants, sneakers, and a dark tunic lettered with the words that serve as title, "Peace Pilgrim." Her eyes have that look of serenity coupled with intensity I crave for myself. I open the book and meet a solitary wanderer who sometime in the middle of her life (at fifty? it doesn't say) stripped away all remnants of her former identity, took the name of Peace Pilgrim, and launched a walking pilgrimage for peace that over the course of three decades led her through every state in the United States and every province of Canada. After twenty-five thousand miles she stopped counting.

Like Margaret, Peace Pilgrim was one of the voluntary homeless. She accepted gifts of food and lodging from people she met along the road; otherwise she slept wherever she found herself at nightfall. She carried and accepted no money, owned nothing but the contents of her pockets and the clothes on her back—whereas I, for all my yearnings, have dispersed my ten thousand possessions through four different states. "I shall remain a wanderer until mankind has learned the way of peace, walking until I am given shelter, fasting until I am given food," she wrote, and joyfully described the "relinquishments" with which she had prepared herself for her pilgrimage: of self-will, of the feeling of separateness, of all attachments ("No one is truly free who is still attached to material things, or to places, or to people"), and of every "negative feeling," including worry.

Wrapped up in my manuscript, embroiled in a divorce, anxious about my children, immersed in a new love affair, I realize how far I am from those purifying relinquishments that plunged me into life on the nubble.

By late July the decorative apricot trees all over Santa Fe begin dropping their ripe fruit on the ground, where they're mostly left to rot. Such waste is unendurable—especially since these lush fruits, unlike the bland ones in stores, are bursting with the same dense flavor as dried apricots. Surreptitiously I begin to harvest them from gutters or the occasional branch hanging over a wall into public domain; but after I learn that fallen apricots are considered as great a nuisance as dandelions, I do it openly. Several homeowners actually invite me into their yards to pick their excess fruit; one sets a ladder against a tree for me. I activate my kitchen, filling the freezer with tarts and turnovers, chutneys and jams, in preparation for my lover's visit.

The kitchen is large and well appointed, and soon I'm conducting experiments with the chiles, purslane, squash, and tomatillos from the Indian market, herbs and fruits from the yard. At first I ignore the string of shiny electric devices for grating, mixing, whipping, juicing, popping, steaming, grinding, brewing, and sharpening that stand ever ready to devour energy, obviate skills, and drown out the sound of cicadas. But some refuse to be ignored: supplies of boiling hot water and of ice cubes bully me by automatically replenishing themselves whenever a drop is used—the very essence of waste. Eventually, curiosity tempts me to give the more outrageous appliances a try. An automatic breadmaker, heavy and loud, adds to the insult of uniformly ugly little cylindrical loaves the injury of usurping the pleasures of kneading and punching down. Though the accompanying booklet boasts, "5 MINUTES TO AUTOMATED FREEDOM COMPARED TO THE 4-HOUR MANUAL METHOD," the machine actually takes the same four hours from beginning to end to produce a loaf of bread. Touting ignorance as bliss, the booklet promises that "you don't need to know anything"—"just spend 5 minutes dumping in the ingredients and over the next 4 hours the breadmaker will do everything else for you automatically"—and even suggests spending your "saved" time watching the machine at work: "It's fun to gather your friends around to watch the bread knead, rise and bake." Similarly, the cumbersome Cuisinart loses out to a simple chef's knife on efficiency, aesthetics, pleasure, and even time if I include cleaning up. I retire the devices to their cupboards.

AT last Charles arrives—in a big hat. He brings a bottle of bubbly and a basketball. How tall, fair, gentle he is!—I'd almost forgotten. When he bends to kiss me, heaving that familiar, effervescent sigh, I'm once more disarmed by his sweetness. Though we know each other to our bones, we're strangers; he keeps asking me, "And what would you like to do now?" He's game to try the foods I find growing in the yard; I'm game to shoot baskets with him at a local playground.

On August 6 of that summer, the fortieth anniversary of the bombing of Hiroshima, we set off early for a protest at Los Alamos, the world's chief nuclear-weapons research laboratory and the birthplace of the Bomb. We drive into the purple mountains, switching off at the wheel every half hour, there's so much to see. Pueblos nestled in the high mesas, rocks shaped like camels or dinosaurs, dry arroyos snaking off through red canyons, stairs leading nowhere, golden expanses of yellow chamiza, gnarled juniper, piñon, and cacti, silver meadows of sage. Whenever we pull over, a frosting of wildflowers comes into focus, like the dots in pointillist paintings. Then, book in hand, I invoke the magical names—owl's foot, fairy trumpet, locoweed, said to drive cattle mad.

"If you really want to see something, we should go cross-country for a while," suggests Charles, as I pull out of the truck stop where we had huevos rancheros for breakfast. He kindly offers to drive. I turn the car onto the first promising jeep track, like a horny lover in search of a secluded spot. In the middle of nowhere, as I slow down to give Charles the wheel, I see him leaning into the window, finger pointing. "Stop slowly," he whispers. "*Slowly*. Look!"

A hundred yards ahead an animal is coming our way—tall, substantial, long-tailed, and—the word pops into my head—*canine*.

"What is it?" I whisper.

"A coyote."

I cut the motor and roll to a slow stop. The coyote saunters toward us jauntily, as if we've pulled onto its property and it's coming out to investigate. As quietly as I can I get out of the car, walk around to the passenger side, and like an innocent wayfarer matter-of-factly seeking directions take two friendly steps toward the animal, holding out my hand, palm up. Reading me perfectly, the coyote keeps coming until it's standing directly before me, sniffing my hand. It has a long snout, erect ears, a shiny brown coat, and a tail thick as a muff. Our eyes meet. The coyote cocks its head to one side and nods, inviting me to pet it—as a potentate might invite a suitor to kiss his hand. For a full minute we stand together like that, the coyote tall and erect,

I lightly stroking its cocked head without a flicker of fear.

The coyote looks me once more in the eyes, then, to the flutelike signal of a meadowlark, abruptly turns and trots back through the high waving grasses.

Back in the car I slouch in my seat, replaying the encounter while sweet-tempered Charles negotiates the rough terrain full of ruts and pits and small rocks that fly up under the old Chevy to bang noisily on the bottom of the chassis. Not all the dogs of my childhood and adulthood had prepared me for this.

ON the highway heading west I take the wheel again. Soon the wild beauty of the canyons is caged behind miles of ominous barbed wire. High-voltage cables, antennas, radar towers disfigure the sky, and signs threatening KEEP OUT! WARNING! NO TRESPASSING! litter the land. The closer we draw to Los Alamos, the more sinister grows the scenery until we're in a different world from the one we left two hours before. Isolated on a mountainside surrounded by deep canyons that carry lethal wastes to the increasingly radioactive Rio Grande, the lab poisons everything. Gradually it's coming out that traces of plutonium contaminate the local chiles and the catfish of Cochiti Lake; downstream from the lab are radioactive peach trees; there are traces of tritium in the canyon's honeybees.

Once we're through the security gates I see barely a dozen demonstrators, though the event has been well publicized. In Boulder only months before, there were hundreds of us, mostly young; now there are only a handful, mostly middle-aged and old, so few there's a soldier to guard each of us.

Beside me, Charles, trim and confident, stands grimly eye to eye with a young MP; on my other side, a gray-haired woman in her late sixties with crinkles around her eyes smiles benevolently up at her soldier. She's dressed in a navy-blue sweat suit and sneakers; the small hands holding up her handmade REMEMBER HIROSHIMA sign are crisscrossed with puffy veins, and suddenly I wonder—is it Peace Pilgrim?

I try not to stare, but my eyes keep returning to that open flower of a face. Finally I sidle up to her and ask straight out. But the woman only laughs. "Peace Pilgrim? You should be so lucky! We could use her today. But I'm afraid it's only us."

Us. I take in our raggedy band, wondering why we're so few. Even if the young aren't particularly interested, there are plenty of older ones for whom Hiroshima is a central event of their lives. And though we're only slowly finding out how recklessly we're heating up the planet, tearing holes in the sky, extinguishing entire species, still, for forty years it's been common knowledge that someone might blow up the world. Is it the remoteness of this history-damaged site that's kept people away? Or the famously apathetic times?

"Anyway, didn't Peace Pilgrim pass away a while back?" asks her double.

Of course!—the book was a memorial assembled by her friends. I've allowed myself to be thrown off by my growing sense of her generic presence in the guise of other gray-haired pilgrims in tennis shoes taking her place. The band of daring old ladies in tennis shoes. Like Margaret, who at this very moment is no doubt carrying on somewhere. And me too, already taken for one by those girls on the nubble, though I'm not halfway through my fifties and my hair has hardly any gray. And holding my sign on top of that mesa where the atom was unleashed, holy land where for millennia Native Americans have lived by the deep knowledge that everyone and everything is connected, I recognize the mortal danger in the illusion of separation.

It is precisely this perception that comes back to me the following year when Clara bursts in with news of the stunning nuclear accident in the Ukrainian town of Chernobyl. I remember the exact moment: I'm propped up in bed in my Chautauqua cottage correcting the galleys of my new book, which the publisher, to my vast relief, accepted, even managing to sell translation rights in several languages. As Clara speaks, the awful recurring fantasy that made me weep when the children were young comes flashing back: they're at school when the Bomb explodes and I can't get to them. I try, but all the roads are blocked with the rubble of fallen buildings; I can't get anywhere near the school. I see other children, parents vainly searching. Charred bodies, severed limbs. And all the time I'm struggling to get to my children I imagine them calling out for me . . .

I try to shake the image from my mind while Clara reports the details. Chernobyl? Chernobyl? I don't understand her. Such an unfamiliar name—we can barely pronounce it. Then I remember how Rocky Flats and Los Alamos too once seemed remote places by my provincial lights until they were suddenly revealed to stand at the center of the world, a straight line connecting each one to the other and to each of us, like moonbeams on water connecting the eyes of every viewer directly with the moon.

Soon, more than metaphor connects me to Chernobyl. When my French publisher asks to see me about the new book, I agree to fly to Paris as soon as school lets out. Since Charles has a technical conference in Berlin on art restoration, we arrange to spend a few days together in Budapest, city of some of my ancestors.

From the tall French windows of the fourth-floor room in our shabby, once elegant hotel we look down on a bridge across the Danube, no longer blue, bordered by a twisty skein of trolley tracks. For centuries people have been coming to this famous "Spa Capital of the World" to take the cure, and our hotel, we discover, is renowned for its healing thermal swimming pool and medicinal baths. We launch each day by making love on faded satin pillows to the clang and bustle of the trolley below, take breakfast in our room off gilt-edged porcelain dishes that don't match, then descend to the baths in the hotel basement. We splash in the mosaic-decorated pool filled to the brim with sulfurous water so buoyant with healing minerals that even the knottiest bodies are able to float. These waters are nothing like the sterilized chlorinated fluids of our health clubs and public pools; the very notion that unknown active impurities smelling faintly like rotten eggs may contain healing properties, or that ailing people should bathe together, is alien to a country that developed the Dustbuster and the atom bomb. But I've reached the age of living dangerously.

We sign up for massages. In the women's steam room large nude females with colossal buttocks, hanging breasts, and rippled thighs walk about freely. When my name is called, I'm ushered down a white-tiled corridor into a high-ceilinged room where two red-faced muscular women in white coats collaborate on my small foreign body. They lay me on a gurney, pull and stretch my limbs, turn me over, hose me down, taking turns massaging my muscles—one slowly kneading my flesh with the heels of her hands, the other drumming it rapidly with the bony sides of hers—until my body tingles with all the new energy I need for another day of walking the streets.

Afterward, as we're about to leave the hotel, a friend of Charles's from the conference phones to offer to squire us around the city for a day. A Hungarian engineer who has settled in the States, Laz is here with his wife, Marie, on their annual visit to his family, staying in the very apartment where he grew up. I propose that we meet at the central market, not far from our hotel, early the following morning. To me, the farmers' market is the gut of a city and, because food is so immediately accessible, circulating through the bloodstream to transform your very cells, it's the most direct way I know to get intimate with a place. When I'm traveling, there are never enough meals to satisfy me. I want to sample everything, from the simplest fare to the most elaborate specialties, experiencing the entire food establishment and underground, markets great and small, street stalls, grocery stores, supermarkets, specialty shops (I once saw a tiny shop in Geneva that carried nothing but goat cheeses—more than a hundred kinds), prepared foods local, regional, international, universal. And restaurants—from street-corner venders to cafés and bistros, right on up (if I could only afford them) to the most celebrated establishments of the "highest" cuisine. My chief frustration at a foreign market is that I have no place to cook the enticing wares for sale but must restrict myself to the pleasures of the eye and what can be eaten out of hand in a park or hotel room.

The next morning at the market there's no sign of Charles's friends. Perhaps they've overslept? When Charles offers to wait outside for them and find me later, I kiss him gratefully and hurry through the iron gates.

The market is housed in one of those great nineteenth-century structures of steel and glass enclosing enormous expanses of open space like the imperial railroad stations of large European cities. Situated in the center of town close to the Danube on which boats have been bringing food from the countryside to the city for a thousand fat years and lean years, it has survived recent decades of austerity and scarcity to become at the time of our visit a showpiece of Central European agriculture. My plan is to walk once quickly through, beginning at the outer rim and spiraling toward the center, trying to get the layout firmly in mind before deciding what to skip over and where to dawdle. But as I start to circle the huge perimeter, walking among the endless displays of food arranged in tempting pyramids, I quickly lose my purpose and begin to linger. Here are foods I have never seen the likes of before. Salmon-colored melons the size of basketballs, plump bronze cherries, shimmering currants as large as Concord grapes, transparent green gooseberries, mountains of paprika, barrels of bay, burlap bags full of spices and herbs, dried and fresh, hazelnuts, walnuts, legumes in endless variety, countless seeds of poppy, fennel, caraway, and dill. Here are heavy squashes, huge pink cabbages, tender brussels sprouts growing in spirals around long woody stalks, and greens completely new to me smelling of the wild countryside. I want to filch and sample each unknown leaf—broad, flat, curly, or bladed, green, silver, purple, or brown. I want to pinch and squeeze and fondle everything.

Next I come to counters and cases where prepared foods—breads, pastries, pâtés, terrines, meat pies, salamis, and sausages—are displayed by muscular chefs in white coats. Then come butcher stalls with carcasses hanging from giant hooks, some with their heads, pelts, or feathers still in place; here are rows of red hams hanging on strings, crocks of pickled heads and tails, smoked feet. Then the game exhibits, ranging from dozens of tiny bite-sized birds tied together at their heads, fanning out into stars, to great long-snouted boars. Stalls for innards—tripes, kidneys, lungs, hearts, brains, and livers, including that most prized offal of all, the pale fois gras—goose livers, plump as cows' tongues, which are shipped from Hungary all over Europe and the world. And now the cheeses, aged, smoked, fresh, herbed; slabs of butter, canisters of milk, and silver urns of thick fresh cream. In my excitement I lose my way, circling ever more slowly, barely able to pull myself from one exhibit to the next until, at the very heart of the market, I come upon the prize: mushrooms.

Wild mushrooms! Never did I dream there could be so many kinds. There, laid out on three long tables arranged in a giant horseshoe, is a dizzying array of wild fungi, some as large as sunflowers, some as tiny as a fingernail paring. How pale and lifeless seem our ordinary cultivated mushrooms beside these mysterious, often brilliantly colored wild species. Besides the familiar buff or gray, there are mushrooms of bright orange, yellow, pale rose, pink, red, raven, purest white. There are mushrooms shaped like trumpets, tiny bells, toadstools, pancakes, potato chips, hats, nails, birds, tears, paws, claws. Each kind is piled in a great tumbling mound, behind each mound is an identifying document with an official inspection stamp, behind each document is a pair of balance scales, and behind each pair of scales stands a black-clad peasant, sometimes a man but more often a woman in babushka and apron, watching perplexed or bemused as I, ignoring their low, incomprehensible pitches, circle the long tables, barely able to keep my hands off the wares.

"Here you are!" cries Charles. "We've been looking all over for you." He grabs my elbow to introduce me to Laz and Marie.

Laz pumps my hand in a blustering manner that sends his straight hair bobbing over his ruddy face. He waves away the mushrooms, asking if I've seen the magnificent displays of goose livers. Not, he insists, pâtés or terrines of liver but whole livers—fresh, fat, heavy, creamy pink: "the real thing." Never, he proclaims, has he seen such magnificent large specimens.

Marie, a soft-spoken blond nurse in her sixties, puts her hand on her husband's arm to calm him. She laughs apologetically at his enthusiasm, but I'm charmed. Recognizing in Laz a kindred passion, I conceive a plan. Instead of stifling our fantasies, why not act on them? Why not, I propose, each buy our heart's desire, take it back to their apartment, and cook it for lunch?

Reluctant glances are exchanged; but when I volunteer to do the cooking, they soften. Laz rushes off in search of the perfect goose liver. Marie selects a fantasy concoction for our salad. Charles buys strudels—prune, cherry, and poppyseed—for dessert, and sweet butter, and crusty bread. Together they choose the wines while I select the mushrooms, ten different kinds.

Some of them look like the puffballs, chanterelles, and wood ears I've seen in the island woods, but they might be anything. Though Laz reads the names off the documents, they're untranslatable and don't register. I want to taste and compare every kind, but the venders won't sell them in small enough quantities to make a larger selection feasible. Even ten kinds is probably overdoing it.

Laz's borrowed kitchen is a small square cheerful room just large enough for the basic appliances plus a wooden table with four matching chairs. The two-burner stove is more than adequate once Laz's mother, summoned for a moment from her downstairs rooms, shows us how to light the oven.

The afternoon sunlight flows in through the window as I slice, then sauté the mushrooms, species by species, in a large buttered skillet. The others wash the vegetables, open the wines, build the salad, cut the bread. Marie carves radishes into flowers and arranges them prettily on a plate with salt and olives. Exercising cook's prerogative, I sample each kind of mushroom as I go before slipping them into a low oven to stay warm while I sauté the next kind. Finally, I slice and cook the goose liver according to Laz's mother's instructions. So fat are these prized organs that the minute the meat hits the pan it begins to melt; after a bit the skillet fills with goose fat in which the thick slices gently fry until the pink has faded to milky white.

Dividing the treasures evenly among the plates, I place the fois gras in the center, then distribute the mushrooms around it, each kind in a separate mound. The subtle blending of colors ranging from creamy white through buff, tan, gray, and black makes the spread look like some prize high-fashion photograph—almost too gorgeous to eat. Nevertheless, we take our seats and raise our glasses in the first of many toasts that transform us, as we progress through this most memorable meal, from four transients accidentally met in Budapest to comrades of the gut. After restoring the kitchen to its earlier state (now enhanced by a large jar of goose fat for Laz's mother), we sit in the living room drinking wine, trading the stories of our lives. It's an intimacy of a single day, but what more can new friendship want than good conversation and a perfect meal?

CHARLES and I have tickets to a concert of Mozart violin sonatas in a renowned Baroque recital hall. In the rain, we offer to share our taxi with another concertgoer from our hotel, a woman with the World Health Organization in Geneva, now in Budapest taking the cure for a painful arthritic condition. We arrange to meet again after the concert to share another taxi back to the hotel. But reluctant to end an exhilarating evening (the performers, one very young and one very old, were both virtuosi), we stop in a café before going home.

Over coffee, the conversation turns to Chernobyl, so recent and so nearby that it's still on everyone's lips. Unaware of how we've spent the day and thinking to reassure us, our new friend announces that, contrary to common opinion, most foods are again perfectly safe to eat, with one exception. Wild mushrooms continue to be heavily contaminated by radiation. Upon inspection, every single truckload that's arrived at the border for export since the disaster has been turned back as unacceptable for human consumption.

Charles's animated eyes widen to reveal familiar dramatic rings of white around the blue as we exchange a silent look. What is there to say? The concert is still reverberating in our ears and the damage is done.

PART THREE

The World

TEN

GLORIOUSLY muscled youths haul up the gangplank, mothers clamp their hands over children's ears while the boat whistle bellows and we leave the port. Seated on deck I wrap my knitted scarf twice around my neck, tilt my head toward the sun, and suck into my nostrils the stimulating harbor smells: salt, oil, iodine, fish. After two years apart, Jerry and I finally signed a divorce settlement that gave us each what we most wanted: the apartment to him and, except for a week each summer when he was free to visit, the nubble to me. Now my body welcomes every roll and pitch of the stubby *Island Romance* ferrying me back to my nubble.

Talk aboard is of Chernobyl—that, and a disturbing new study of the island's wells revealing groundwater contamination. I eavesdrop anxiously. Drinking the rain instead of well water, perhaps I'm safe. But then I hear how clouds circle the world, transporting dust from everywhere, even Chernobyl.

When we enter Hussy Sound I follow my fellow passengers down the stairs to the cabin below. Word is out: with a hole newly discovered in the ozone layer, humans must avoid the sun.

• • •

SOMETHING'S wrong with the apple tree. I see it the moment I hit the beach. The lower branches, still sporting a few blossoms, are lavishly leaved in a spring-green veil, but the top half of the tree is bare, as if beheaded, the branches naked and exposed. My heart lurches; I turn away. When I look again the same shock assaults me. I head for the cove to inspect the damage.

The leaves of the lower branches are crawling with sinister brown caterpillars gorging themselves on chlorophyll, my tree's life's blood. My only apple tree, bearer of fragrant blossoms in spring and major nourishment in fall, home to successive flocks of warblers, swallows, and finches, familiar silhouette on the horizon when I reach the beach, beacon of home, venerable connection with bygone orchards—stripped! And spread across the top on the outermost twigs far out of my reach is a line of deathly gray web-like nests, each enclosing a writhing mass of larvae.

"In the fight between you and the world, back the world," writes Kafka. For two anxious weeks I try, stoically watching the nubble's only tree defoliate until not one leaf remains. The inch-long larvae, with their segments daintily outlined in ermine white against nut-brown fur with two orange spots on their backs, spread out across the entire nubble—nestling in the soft new growth between the branches of the bayberry bushes, stripping the wild roses before they even have a chance to bud.

Then one morning I wake to feel one crawling up my arm. I open my eyes to see two more on the bedsheet, another on my pillow, and several moving slowly down the inside of the window screen. I fling them from my bed and in that moment resolve to fight back, vowing death to another species. So much for passive acceptance.

My first day of battle, still squeamish, I carry the caterpillars I collect down to the beach and try to burn them; the second day, experimental, I try to drown them in a bucket of seawater. But they crawl away from the fire and wriggle on top of the water. On the third day I devise a foolproof method: stomp them to death. I gather ten or twenty in my hand where, curled like fiddleheads, they nestle quietly until I find a flat bit of earth for a killing field; then I lay them in a heap, cover them with leaves, and squash them underfoot. I find I can kill five hundred an hour, which becomes my daily quota: a hundred on the way to the outhouse, a hundred as I descend the stairs, another hundred or two on the path toward South Beach when I go for the mail, and another on my way to Dedgers for seaweed. Nothing moral or personal, you understand; we're a long way from those sixteenth-century public trials at which horses and pigs were sentenced to death for destructive behavior; but I can't stand by helplessly watching the nubble perish. As I transfer the larvae from bush to palm, counting as I go, the rhythmic process begins to feel almost like collecting rose hips or raspberries—one more disciplined practice of attention; only, instead of tranquil, I am agitated. I reserve my oldest sneakers for the job and ignore what clings to my sole.

Once the tide comes in, you can't reach the treasures in the cove. Now I fear the tide is coming in for me. Even on the nubble where the timeless blue water meets the endless blue sky I know the law of the world: *everything changes.* Know that every year brings its own peculiar mix of disasters and blessings. Yet never have the changes seemed so ominous. Ever since Richard Mann leaned back on his heels and reassured me about mussels and clams, I'd thumbed my nose at red-tide warnings; but this is a new kind of danger—manmade and terrible.

Daily, the news grows worse: Casco Bay's seemingly pristine waters are pronounced the most polluted on the Eastern Seaboard, and its air—always so pure, clean, invigorating—is revealed to be nearly the worst in the country, carrying the industrial smog of greater Boston directly into our island lungs. The rain I've been complacently drinking for years becomes suspect when I learn that the asphalt roofing shingles it washes may possibly be toxic, like most petroleum products.

In a brutally hot summer with a record number of record-breaking days, producing the worst drought nationwide since the Dust Bowl of 1934, when sewage and hospital waste foul beaches on both coasts just when people melting with heat most need their beaches for cooling off, when dolphins and sea lions wash up dead in unprecedented numbers, when a notable scientist warns the world in the pages of *Time* that anyone would be "crazy" to eat liver of lobster caught near urban areas or any freshwater fish at all, when research on hepatitis B renders all bivalves henceforth suspect—that summer I seriously question my safety. I worry about the mussels that have set me free and the mussel broth I use as my basic cooking stock. I worry about my vegetables—my salads, fruits, and potherbs—which, though free of pesticides and chemical fertilizers, are watered by the same suspect rain that carries fallout from halfway around the world. And for the first time I worry about the seaweeds bathed in now-questionable waters and coated with suddenly suspect salts. (The label on a loaf of good bread brought out to me by a new Portland friend, Linda, claims to use "only purified water, the quality found in the healthiest of springs, and natural mineral salt, NOT sea salt.

This natural mineral salt was born 50 million years ago, before pollutants contaminated our seas.")

In my two-year absence can the seven fat years have come to an end, inaugurating seven lean? Am I being tested (or punished) for having so brazenly embraced the principle of *amor fati*? I recall the punch line to the old joke about the farmer weaning his horse from food: "Just as I had him trained to do without oats altogether, he up and died!"

Not that my food supply seems worse than elsewhere, but less and less does it seem better. A new, disturbing thought gathers and lengthens: the total interconnectedness of things, the vision of unity and abundance that I first saw on the subway in a rapturous flash, means that if we all share in the blessing of life, we also share in the curse. To experience fully the intensity of each moment must mean to experience its anguish as well as its bliss. Margaret's faith that what happens anywhere happens everywhere means that *everywhere* includes this blessed island. Even the life-giving sun itself is being accused and feared like a violent criminal on the loose.

When I stumble upon a syringe amid a small tangle of transparent plastic hospital gloves washed up on the very spot where, half a decade before, I harvested my first crop of fishermen's gloves, I hear the serpent of doubt hiss. Innocent intentions yield such perverse results: hospitals dedicated to sterility inadvertently spread germs; the very agricultural technology that once promised to feed the hungry and enhance earthly life turns out to destroy the soil, pollute the rivers and oceans. Despite the Green Revolution, at every moment somewhere on Earth there is famine, and fifty thousand people die daily of malnutrition or starvation—on a *good* day.

Have I been fooling myself all along, or has something

critically changed? Has my sojourn out in the world enabled me to see at last what I've been blind to, or has history finally landed on this remote tip of an island?

I remember how long it took me when I began gathering mussels to see their predators, the green crabs that share their habitat—except when I went crabbing and became momentarily blind to mussels. Like the blindness that comes from too much light, mine came from the sheer intensity of my focus, the ardor of my wish. Not until I understood the inextricable connection between mussels and crabs was I able to see both crabs and mussels at once. Just so, now that I've discovered the island's connection to the world, I see it everywhere.

The inhabited islands of these coastal waters proceed with their destined decline, down to fourteen year-round communities from three hundred at the turn of the century. And not only human communities: the chorus of songbirds to which I wake each morning is performed by an ensemble a fraction the size of the one that once sang the day's overture. The sandpipers I used to count in groups of ten to twenty daily along the shore now appear irregularly, usually in pairs or trios, sometimes alone, never more than six. This year the barn swallows have forsaken the outhouse to nest elsewhere—though I take comfort in their occasional return to the front-deck railing to sun themselves, and in the gathering armada of ducks, which seems undiminished as it moves slowly past uninhabited Marsh Island. (Marsh Island itself, home in the Fifties to an enterprising hermit who lived in a lean-to and rowed his homegrown vegetables to market, is now covered with poison ivy and guano.) Once I counted thirty-seven chattering purple finches in the apple tree, arranging themselves like a shimmering boa draped across the top fringe of leaves where now obtrude nothing but ten menacing, unreachable insect nests, hostile outposts of the new occupation forces. As I pluck and stomp, pluck and squash, I wonder if there may not be a connection, if the occasional caterpillar of years past had perhaps been picked off and contained by the abundant birds. In an experiment on a four-level food chain consisting of trout, dragonflies, midge larvae, and algae in a California river, researchers discovered that removing the top predator, the trout, enabled the dragonflies to multiply unchecked and consume all the midge larvae, leaving the algae, deprived of a predator, free to increase a hundredfold. Soon the fishless river was clogged with dense mats and braids of algae bloom. Similarly, when the top predator, a starfish, was removed from a rich intertidal community of limpets, chitons, snails, barnacles, bivalves, and other invertebrates, the highly diverse community quickly collapsed into one of monotonous simplicity as mussels took over. With fewer birds on the island, perhaps the caterpillars will triumph. If so, I reflect in bitter consolation as I carry out my sabotage, they are doomed to undermine their own hegemony like every imperial power before them. Should they strip this poor defenseless nubble of every last leaf, they must themselves eventually starve, or depart for other worlds, new conquests.

An itchy rash erupts on my neck. The red skin is on fire. Sunburn? Poison ivy? Allergy? I rub on soothing calamine lotion, then don a cotton turtleneck to keep myself from scratching. When the babies of the renters across the beach come down with a worse rash all over their bodies, I donate the calamine, wondering if our rashes are related. Their mother carries her infant to a clinic in Portland where he's tentatively diagnosed with bedbug bites, and in a panic she leaves the island five days early. After they've gone I notice with alarm that the pear tree beside their cottage is also infested with the blight. The changes are out of control. After two weeks of battle there are still hundreds of thousands, perhaps millions of caterpillars left to go. I see them all over the nubble gorging themselves, crawling on the decks, rendering my paltry five hundred bodies a day a useless joke, a mere token of my commitment to struggle. But as Rabbi Tarfon said five hundred years ago, in words presently mounted on my wall, "It is not required of you that you complete the task but neither are you free to abandon it."

If the songbird population has thinned, the boats in the cove have multiplied. One Sunday I count dozens of motorboats, sailboats, yachts, sloops, racing boats—all except lobster boats, which seem to grow fewer every year. And not only in Shark Cove. The governor's office reports that the harbors of the Maine coast are so crowded with pleasure craft that the lines of lobster buoys are constantly being cut by careless boaters, and soon there may no longer be room for fishing boats at all. In Portland the working waterfront has given way to condos and developments; tall new bank buildings fill the skyline of the Old Port; the boat industry is a shambles, and in some places the lobster and fishing hauls have been halved. The damage is already done, the direction set: what else can it mean that in the inflated Eighties land values more than triple in a mere five years? The boom roars through New England like thunder, cursing the islanders, whose livings come mainly from the sea, with punishingly high taxes that threaten to strip them of their homes.

On our island the big news of the previous summer had been the "million-dollar house," a large window-clad mansion with an old-fashioned widow's walk on top, built on a pristine isolated point. The builder, a developer from New

Jersey, flew in his own construction crew, bypassing the local carpenters. Islanders gathered around to gawk at the appliances delivered by ferry to the dock: washer, dryer, dishwasher, garbage disposal, compactor, and jumbo redwood hot tub, all of the most elaborate and expensive brands. People shook their heads over the white wall-to-wall carpeting and the shatterproof glass with which every window had to be replaced in order to withstand the vibrations of the helicopter the owners used for their long commute.

But the million-dollar house is nothing compared to what might be coming. Already a large development of condos is going up on nearby Ruby Island. Our island, about three miles long and one mile wide at its widest, approximately nine hundred acres, seems a prime target for attack—especially the old navy property confiscated during World War II and later held by a series of land speculators. The giant holding company that presently owns it has already begun petitioning the government for permission to build, despite mighty local efforts to stop them. How long before they win?

In all the years I've been coming to Long Island it never occurred to me to explore the rest of it (much less visit the other islands on the ferry line), since there was still so much to uncover exactly where I was. Within walking distance of any spot on Earth there's probably more than enough mystery to investigate in a lifetime; for that reason, while I lived in Boulder I never spent time in legendary Denver, though it was only a couple hours' drive from home. But when Charles, an explorer, comes out to visit, we pack a lunch early Saturday morning and set off to circumnavigate the island.

Instead of heading across South Beach toward the road where the mailbox stands, as I do most days, we set off in the other direction, across Singing Sand Beach at the edge of Shark Cove, and then over the rocks along the irregular shoreline. We climb up granite bluffs overlooking vast beds of mussel and seaweed, from which we search the horizon for unknown islands. We pass rocky beaches, secret inlets, muddy coves, dark hidden sea caves pounded by surf. At every turn new ecologies open at our feet, and I fill my pockets and backpack with interesting new specimens. As we hug the shore, curving around a bend every few yards, the traditional points of the compass become useless, even disorienting—such is the nature of an island. (On the volcanic islands of Hawaii, for instance, the directions are *mauka*, toward the mountains, *makai*, toward the sea, and, on Oahu, *Ewa*, toward the town of Ewa, and *Koko*, toward Koko Head Crater—more stable designations than N, S, E, W.)

Eventually we come to a road that leads us alongside a large marshy pond covered with white and pink water lilies. Toads hop among the lily pads, and waterfowl I haven't seen around the nubble duck among the reeds. I want to sample the tubers of the water lilies, said to be, like yams, both sweet and starchy, but the marsh is enclosed by a chain-link fence, suggesting that it's probably part of the navy property. With many of the islands of Casco Bay pocked by bunkers, forts, and towers built as military installations for harbor defense ever since the Revolution, this is a familiar annoyance. During World War II the nubble itself was used as a lookout station, whose lonely sentry my nearest neighbor (now in her eighties) used to visit at his post with her toddlers (now middle-aged, married, and gone). On the front side of the island, most of the grandest waterfront houses, which had given Long Island its panache back in the 1890s when it was a popular summer resort, were confiscated and bulldozed by the navy. To this day, the fence encloses about two hundred acres containing huge hazardous underground oil-storage tanks, used during the war to fuel the North Atlantic Fleet. Ironically, it is the prohibitive cost of removing the tanks to make the area safe for habitation that keeps the developers at bay.

When the sun is directly overhead, we leave the coast for a shaded inland road. Now another world spreads out before us. We're surprised to find such diversity in an area a fraction the size of Manhattan. The island's population, one hundred fifty swelling to nearly a thousand in summer, is spread out sparsely along the shore, or perched in houses on the crest of the ridge to capture the views, or tucked away in the woods at the end of dirt roads. Like the hodgepodge of island cars, these houses—ingenious and eccentric, locally designed and built—are greatly varied: besides the New England saltboxes and patched fishing shacks, there are A-frames, lean-tos, an octagonal house, a hexagonal one, a Tower House (converted from a former navy lookout tower), a stilt house, a chalet, a mansion or two. Beamed high-pitched roofs, shingle or board-and-batten sheathing, wraparound porches, widow's walks, old stained-glass windows, new glass curtains facing the sea. Here and there a porch is piled high with lobster traps or a yard is completely planted in flowers.

When we come to the small cemetery beyond the school, we turn in and eat our lunch there. Afterward, encircled by pines, we wander among the eighteenth- and nineteenth-century headstones marking the graves of teenage mothers dead in childbirth, some buried beside their infants, of brave fishermen taken by storms, of patriarchs and matriarchs and beloved sons, of successions of families whose descendants down the generations still pepper the island with their surnames: Cushing and Gomez, Griffin and Doughty. Luckier they than the native settlers of the Abenaki tribe who, displaced by white settlers beginning in 1623, have left no known descendants on the island's rolls, though occasionally someone digging in the sand will turn up a flint arrowhead or a remnant of their huge shell middens still scattered along the coast.

The backpack is lighter now that we've eaten, and we leave the cemetery refreshed. We walk on through two small clusters of cottages, the East End and the West End. Mansard roofs and gingerbread trim reflect the island's Victorian heyday when steamships brought summer visitors here from all the major cities of the East. There were once three separate boat landings, several general stores and restaurants, three substantial hotels. Cabanas ranged all along the dunes of South Beach, one of the finest white-sand beaches in the state. The Casco Bay Hotel held elaborate outdoor clambakes, serving lobster and clams, potatoes and corn, every day of the summer, three sittings each. But after the automobile made mainland beaches readily accessible, the island fell out of favor with vacationers, and eventually into decline. The largest, most luxurious hotel burned to the ground, the smaller ones folded, and the navy's occupation completed the island's commercial doom.

The sun crosses the sky, the tide recedes, but on we walk until, on a far shore at the back of the island, we come to a small harbor of fishing boats. Though I've never been here before, the oversized flagpole, the tumbledown bait shack, the curve of the shore look oddly familiar. Then gradually I realize that this point, situated at one tip of a bay that curves into Shark Cove, is visible on a clear day across the water from my own front deck.

How different it looks from the other side! Here, opposite

my own, is another nubble jutting into the sea; only, here floating moorings bob in the water in place of lobster buoys, the sand is coarse and tan, not fine enough to sing, and instead of the wild spinach and dusty miller fringing my beach, a wide expanse of fragrant sea lavender grows. A sign proclaims the house atop this nubble to be *The Nubble House*, reducing mine to namelessness.

Slowly, eyes to the ground, I walk to the water's edge until, looking abruptly up, I find myself staring straight at my cabin. There on a bluff it sits, distant and still, a simple nameless beachhouse beside its jaunty privy, a few quick brushstrokes surrounded by a swath of green. It startles me like a dream recalled. I'm riveted. Is this how the first astronauts felt looking back at Earth? The disorienting jolt is like hearing a lover's name on unexpected lips. With the tide nearly out, the double crescent of South Beach and Singing Sand Beach that separates the nubble from the rest of the island appears larger, making the cabin smaller—an insignificant gray shack as impersonal as a postage stamp. And suddenly I see the nubble as a piece of the ordinary world.

I'm stunned. Is this the true meaning of unity? The wholeness I seek? Is this the meaning of the ancient Jewish philosopher Philo's cryptic line, "The true name of eternity is Today"?

Arriving back home in the late afternoon, I wonder how my outlook will be changed now that I've walked all the way around the world. As I peer across the water toward the harbor, the view is subtly altered; not even the mist settling on the opposite shore can restore its mysterious air of elsewhere. When the double-crested cormorant rapidly flapping its great black wings spread like opera capes to dry in the sun leaves the Schmoos for the other side, I know its destination—just as I know the destination of the housefly kicking and buzzing in the web of a watching spider.

"I'm making spritzers," says Charles, getting out ice for sundowners.

I consider dashing to the beach for dandelion buds and periwinkles for hors d'oeuvres, but the drinks are ready and there isn't time. (Time!—which always slips back in with company.) We carry our glasses to the deck to toast the health of the world, which seems to need a boost, and watch the last of the Saturday sailors, a family of four, collect their picnic things from the beach. The parents slip yellow life jackets over the heads of two bare-bellied children, then pile their gear and garbage into a green dinghy. After the father pushes off and jumps in, the mother rows smoothly out to their boat. By the time they lift anchor and sail away, leaving the empty beach to us, Charles is rubbing my back and I've already forgotten that other nubble across the bay.

We take our buckets to the rocks to gather seaweed and catch crabs for our dinner of crab sandwiches and seaweed salad, which we carry to the beach on a tray and balance on a log. We eat facing the sea while the sun sets behind us and puffy coral clouds slow-dance across the horizon to the rhythm of surf slapping the shore, backing up a chorus of raucous gulls from Obed's Rock, with alternating riffs of alto crow, high reedy gull, and the *kik-kik-kik* of a tern. When the harbor across the bay becomes a string of lights, foghorns take up the bass. We lie on the beach, jamming with the world.

THE next morning Charles picks up the spade he's brought out, along with an assortment of seeds, and breaks ground for a garden behind the outhouse. Deprived of apples and ready to cut back on mussels, I eagerly examine the pictures of gleaming peppers and shiny squash on the seed packets and for the first time hanker for big luscious beefsteak tomatoes. We turn under the brambles and sorrel, break up the fertile earth, and plant the magic seeds.

As soon as Charles leaves, the fridge goes out for good. I use up a whole box of matches relighting it but can't keep it going. Finally I give up. There's almost nothing in it anyway—a few leftovers, four eggs, half a bottle of white wine. From now on, I decide, I'll use powdered milk and get my eggs fresh from Sarah Mann, who raises chickens, and what shellfish I dare to eat can stay cold in the sea till I'm ready to cook them. I rig up a wine cooler out of an abandoned lobster trap that I tie to a shoreline rock, glad of the new opportunity for ingenuity, each exercise of which always makes me feel a little more free.

The garden has an opposite effect. Until now, my garden has been whatever grows. In the wild, whatever is perfectly suited to this sandy soil, this salty air, this rocky coast is what comes up; what can grow will grow. Call it faith, or my anarchist streak, or my trust in the anthropological commonplace that gathering communities have greater leisure than agricultural ones, but I never worried over my crops. Wielding no spade or hoe, planting no seed, thinning no row, I had only to find, protect, husband, and harvest what flourished here. For foraging, the more varied and serendipitous the conditions, the better—like life at its adventurous best; like solitude.

But all this is reversed for a cultivated garden, where not varied but controlled conditions are required. Where every plant to sprout is known in advance because you put it there. Where the exact depth and spacing of the seeds and seedlings are mandated on the packet even unto the quarter inch, and you sow, thin, stake, feed, and harvest according to schedule.

Now all at once my hardy plant world turns delicate on me. Rain, whose presence or absence had always pleased me equally, becomes a matter of grave concern, and, absent rain, I am profligate with water, daily pumping bucketsful for my needy seedlings. Instead of tossing my garbage over the deck, I must tend it in a compost heap. Species with which I'd long lived peacefully, even obliviously, are abruptly transmuted into "pests": I turn against insects, am suspicious of birds. Thinning a patch of seedlings feels risky, treading among the rows positively reckless; no longer can I run to the outhouse heedless of where I step. The poet May Sarton tells her journal: ". . . hardly a day without anxiety about the garden for one reason or another"—and finally I understand her. Elsewhere she writes that a garden is like poetry "in the amount of waste that has to be accepted for the sake of the rare, chancy joy when all goes well."

Waste? Rare, chancy joy? The very separation and compartmentalizing I escaped by coming to the nubble now reproduce themselves inside my garden as I reintroduce *waste* and trade my continuous harvest for *rare, chancy joy*. What was carefree and spontaneous becomes cautious and civilized—like the trade-offs of love, rewarding care, attention, and commitment with certain cultivated delights and enchantments. Now, for the sake of variety, I stake, string, and label a few rows of prestigious seeds and begin each morning with a keen inspection of my privileged plot, checking the conditions of the soil, measuring the vulnerable progress of each germination like an anxious parent. I coddle the beets, radishes, and yellow squash, pamper the chives and basil, overindulge the tomatoes. Ambitious for my charges, I promote the advantage of each with extra water and food, while outside the white string that marks the garden's arbitrary borders weedy barbarians that were once my chosen look on resentfully, planning their attack.

It doesn't take long. "Nothing . . . plants weeds as efficiently as cultivation," writes the weed expert Sarah Stein. Every few days I squat in the rows to pull up the creeping sorrel and pushy charlock that snatch the nutrients from my wards, ignoring the keep-out signs. I toss them behind the lines to join their fellows or set them aside for lunch. A soul divided, I uproot them inside the garden even as I root for them outside.

The task seems increasingly absurd, if not impossible: the weeds of the nubble will take over the garden the minute I turn my back and will be here long after I'm gone. Curly dock seeds, I read, have been known to sprout after seventy years, lamb's-quarters seeds after seventeen hundred, whereas most seeds ordered from a catalogue will be useless after a year or two, and the tomatoes are probably already sterile. Given these unequal forces, why not *love mine enemy*, who just over the border is mine ally?

One morning when I pop a radish bud into my mouth to find my tongue nipped by the familiar zing of charlock, I see the relation clearly. The charlock towering over my radishes just beyond the string even look like radish in stalk, leaf, bud, and flower. Then maybe there's more to radish than root? Later, slicing radishes, stalks and all, into my salad, I consider the charlock stalks which, for all my talk of eating the entire plant, I've been stripping of their treasured flowers and leaves, then tossing out. Now, inspired by radish, I make a meal of a single four-foot charlock stalk—crisp when raw, tender when steamed—gratified that the two cousins, showy degenerate and hardy bumpkin, can reveal each other's neglected qualities, showing me anew the connectedness of things.

I'VE been grieving for weeks over my apple tree, when one day I look down to see a few touches of green rising among the dry branches. Is it elderberry pushing up through the dead wood, or is it possible that now, in the middle of July, when other apple trees on the island are already fruiting, my battle-scarred veteran may be coming back to life? I can't force myself down to the cove to investigate a tree so recently crawling with larvae. But in the following days I see no more caterpillars; the green spreads out to the tips of the highest branches—far too high for elderberry—until by the end of July the entire tree is once again leaved in apple green, looking its normal healthy midsummer self in a non-bearing year. In fact, if I were only then, in late July, arriving on the nubble for a week-long stay, as I had for so many years, I would never suspect what the apple tree had suffered and would probably admire as butterflies the host of white moths now flitting across the brush.

Then how can I know that this year's caterpillar blitz isn't an intermittent part of the tree's life course, like hay fever for Stevie come spring? How presumptuous my claims to knowledge based only on what I see, leaving out what I fail to see. What a slow learner I am! After all, that an organism may spend the energies of its springtime resisting being eaten alive is not unknown to me. And did I not, at fifty, put out a whole new crop of leaves myself?

A letter arrives from the Department of Agriculture, to which I'd fired off a panicky inquiry. Samuel Pratt, entomologist, identifies my enemy as the larva of the browntail moth, whose hairs contain a toxin that can produce a poison-ivy-like rash. He warns me that wind-carried skins and hairs shed by the insects may sometimes affect humans, but usually one must physically handle the caterpillars to get the rash. Making no promises of apples, he assures me that my tree will refoliate in spring and lists two "safe" sprays.

Spray my apple tree? Never! But to keep it alive? Sometimes extraordinary measures must be taken in matters of life and death. It's one thing to hold your faith when everything's going fine, but in this year of so many shattered certainties I don't know what to do. Naturally, I hope my tree will bear again, let me taste again the pies of yore; but as I struggle with this latest challenge to my preconceptions in my ceaseless negotiation with the given, I'm thinking not of fruit but of survival.

ELEVEN

JERRY'S at the nubble with his gang for a week, Charles is back home, and I'm out wandering in the world. I left a bouquet of flowers to welcome Jerry and his new young wife, took a ferry to Portland, and now I'm pushing my shopping cart through a season's worth of errands as I ponder the irony that the divorce which set me free also banishes me from the nubble. Okay, then—I'll use my banishment to pick up survival tips at the annual Common Ground Country Fair, sponsored by the state's organic farmers, where I'm planning to drive tomorrow with Margaret and our Portland friend Linda if it doesn't rain.

On my way from the laundromat to the library, I pass a three-story-high banner announcing "A Celebration of Good Health and Great Food" at the Civic Center. Sponsored by a local supermarket chain to benefit hunger relief, the festival promises all you can eat for three dollars.

It's lunchtime. I'm hungry. I park my cart with the guard and purchase a ticket.

More than a hundred venders fill the giant hall where customers are lined up three or four deep for free samples. Here and there toddlers are having tantrums, but most of the crowd shuffles slowly through the aisles in orderly lines beneath paper streamers, gay balloons, and large TV monitors on which a stream of half-naked dancing girls grind and cavort to the music of four live rock bands alternating on two main stages. Later, Miss America herself is scheduled to make an appearance. Eat this, look like that, goes the subliminal message of the slim young sexy smiling girls.

I'm confused. At every display brochures and flyers tout their wares as "low-calorie," "low-fat," "low-sodium," "diet," "enriched," "nourishing," "vitamin-rich," "protein-packed"—yet they seem to be promoting the usual processed meats, packaged breads, ice creams, doughnuts, candies, sodas, melts. The richer the food, it seems, the more flagrantly it's hawked as healthy, with the richest desserts of all—the cheesecakes, apple pies, and chocolate layer cakes—presented as diet food, guaranteed to slim you down and improve your health (if, parenthetically, you restrict yourself to portions as small as the small print conveying the caveat). If you prefer your fat salty instead of sweet, you can sample chips, crisp noodles, cheese snacks, crackers, fried chicken wings, pork rinds, barbecued ribs, franks, mini-pizzas. Or, for a simple sugar high, with or without caffeine, there are mountains of candies, rivers of chocolate, fountains of red, green, yellow, purple liquids cascading down over ice. Only once at the entire fair do I find a product that invites consumers to "give in to blatant excess"—which I do at once.

When my head is throbbing from the relentless music, and the cigarette smoke is getting to me (or is it the sugar rush?), I snatch one last cookie and head for the door. Clutching a fistful of leaflets on "Cooking with Velveeta" and "Instant Egg Pickup," I ask a guard for the recycle bin. He points toward a row of trash cans, but every one is overflowing with a goop of greasy plates, plastic cups, and garbage. I ask for my cart—"You mean that old-lady cart?" says the well-meaning guard—and leave.

That night I sleep on a futon in Linda's living room; early the next morning we meet Margaret's bus from Boston and head north. Linda drives. We sing. Though we're of three different generations, with almost as many years between Linda and me as between me and Margaret, we find common voice in children's rounds, ballads, and protest songs. Linda and I sing alto harmonies for Margaret's lusty soprano. With her silver hair streaming down her back and her mouth wide open, despite the missing teeth Margaret seems younger than either of us—perhaps immortal.

Gradually the highway crowds up with a caravan of small cars, old pickups, four-wheel drives, VW Bugs—all converging on the fair in Windsor, where bearded farmers in plaid wool jackets and serious boots direct us to park in a converted pasture and hand us programs printed on (recycled) newsprint. We split up, agreeing to meet at the food stalls at lunchtime. Margaret heads for the Whole Life Tent with its Boulderesque workshops in Aura Clearing, Educational Kinesiology, Working with Subtle Energy Fields, and Past Life Therapy. Linda searches out the Folk Art Tent, where demonstrations of tatting, basketry, pot throwing, fly tying, chair caning, and rugmaking alternate through the week. I make a beeline for the Agricultural Tent with its workshops in Food Drying in the Open Air, Salvaging Damaged Fruit, Wild Plants and Their Electrical Fields, Composting, Gathering Roots and Herbs, Garlic & Cousins, Minor Fruits (offered alternately with Major Fruits), Food Politics, Food Abuse, Selecting an Edible Landscape, and the Family Bean.

I'm thrilled to find an entire fair full of people pursuing the very ideals of frugality and harmony I learned at the nubble—folks who raise their own food for the pleasure of it and see no special virtue in bathing every day. Passing among the roving pipers, jugglers, strummers, fiddlers, and the All-Women's Barbershop Chorus, smelling new apples and old manure, I recall the country fairs of my youth, all dedicated to Progress: the Ohio fairs displaying huge tractors and combines, the Danbury Fair to which Jerry and I took our city toddlers to introduce them to cows, the great agricultural fairs of Flaubert and Hardy and Eliot that I attended in my armchair. By contrast, this fair—held at a time when agriculture has turned corporate and chemical, replacing people, crops, and food with machines, outputs, and commodities—is for farmers under pressure and land under siege. Oxen, Draft Horse, and Mule Demonstrations, Manure Pitch-offs, Sheep Shearing Contests, though traditional, here have an edge of defiance to them, an air of organized resistance.

Yet, as I circle the food stalls at lunchtime, I see the fragility of this resistance. Since the entire fair is dedicated to organic husbandry, I'm not surprised that the food offerings are required to be made from certifiably organic ingredients, or that white flour and refined sugar are banned, along with preservatives, hormones, and chemical additives. What surprises me is that alongside the freshly pressed apple cider, steamed corn-on-the-cob, and grilled eggplant there seem to be far more foods masquerading as junk food—or coming as close as they can without actually violating the rules. Two plump sisters dressed in calico dirndls and matching head scarves plunk handfuls of (no doubt whole wheat) dough into great vats of boiling oil, then roll them in (raw) sugar, while beside them a man french-fries (organic) potatoes in a second vat. Soyburgers and not dogs served on airy buns are smothered in fried onions, cheese, salsa, mustard, or topped with baconlike bits. You can munch treacly-sweet seven-grain muffins, lick cones of frozen yogurt dripping with any of half a dozen toppings, swill corn chowder thick with melted cheese, snack on cocoa marble-fudge (brown) rice pudding, crunch two kinds of "Temptress Treats": tofu chocolate bars and carob-covered granola bars. However "natural," "organic," or "unrefined" the ingredients, evidently the major appeal is still to the sweet tooth and salt tongue.

Junk food and health food are cross-dressing—at least when they go to a fair. Is this one more instance of opposites converging, borders blurring, the universe shrinking, as I've begun to notice all around me, even on the island? Is this the underlying meaning of unity? Further evidence that what's happening anywhere will happen everywhere, as Margaret says? Or simply entropy kicking in? I can hardly wait to tell Margaret and Linda, who should be arriving for lunch any minute.

STEVIE once remarked that coming to the island with his father was like visiting an entirely different world from the one I inhabit. Riding back on the ferry, I wonder if a week of Jerry's style has produced some subtle alteration of the nubble's spirit, or perhaps begun some new convergence. Evidently Jerry's had a similar thought, for a note on the kitchen counter accuses me, only half in jest, of placing a hex on the house which gave his entire party an itchy rash that sent them packing after two days.

I'm relieved to see that the telltale signs of another life—ant poison, empty casings of firecrackers, a new bat beside the bed—are nothing but things, after all: inert and disposable. True, the spiderwebs I tried to spare have perished in the zeal of cleanup, the garden is wilting from a rainless week, and the dandelion buds I so zealously picked back have flowered. But the orach has finally entered its long-awaited broccoli phase right on schedule, and on my third day back, after a brief shower, a double rainbow rises out of the ocean to span the entire sky. (Years later, living in Hawaii, I'll see rainbows every day, often double ones; but this is only the third rainbow I've ever seen.) I hurry down the path for a front-row seat.

One of the rainbows is luminous and bright; the other, separated from the first by half a dozen rainbow widths of gray sky, is a smaller, duller mirror image of the first, the colors reversed. As if on cue, two boats, mainsails full, sail slowly across the lighted stage, one under each arch.

After about ten minutes, the colors in the primary rainbow subtly change as the outside band of green gradually takes on alongside it a wide band of violet; then both rainbows begin to vanish. First the shadow rainbow disappears, then the bright one fades from both ends, diminishing to a faint arc high in the sky. A few minutes later it too is gone, and the houselights come up on a plain blue-green day.

Exhilarated, I walk down to the beach to gather greens. Doreen, a local girl Stevie once befriended, sits alone on a rock facing the sea. She's grown into a woman since I last saw her, though her nose is still freckled and her voice high as a child's. "Did you catch that double rainbow?" she asks, full of amazement. When she tells me that this is the first one she's seen though she's lived around here all her life, I invite her to lunch.

We sit on the shady deck cooled by ocean breezes, slowly downing garlicky white-bean soup, a mixed salad of wild greens and garden radishes, corn bread laced with dock seeds, and half a bottle of chablis chilled in a bucket of ocean, while Doreen fills me in on her life. The youngest child in a large family of naturalists (her father is a park ranger, her mother a teacher), she's a junior at a college in Michigan, where she works at a sex-counseling job, and since last winter she has become a vegetarian. She's familiar with some of the wild vegetables we're eating and curious about the rest, especially the seaweeds. I promise to show them to her after lunch.

The conversation grows more lively with each exchange, moving from food to sex to health, then gliding on to pollution, danger, and the Bomb. Doreen speculates that pollution, or fallout from Chernobyl, may have contributed something to the glory of the rainbow, just as sulfurous impurities spewed into the air by distant volcanoes are said to enhance Pacific sunsets.

Being by then a bit tipsy on that rare midday glass of wine, I confide my growing alarm in light of the latest environmental and nuclear revelations.

To which Doreen counters—with a defiant toss of her tight brown curls—that she, on the contrary, is optimistic.

"But the Bomb could fall tomorrow," I point out.

Triumphantly she announces, "It hasn't fallen yet."

I remember the price of such innocence in Budapest, where we gorged ourselves on tainted mushrooms. But seeing Doreen's happy face animated by youth and hope, I sense the irrelevance of opposing her. If our food supply is tainted, you can't tell it from this lunch. Besides, from the set of her jaw I know that nothing I say can dampen her optimism because, Bomb or no, here we are on this radiant afternoon privileged to discuss it.

"If it were to fall right now," says Doreen, "I'd think while it was falling how lucky we are to be having this delightful meal."

"And the rainbow," I add. "Not a bad note to end on if it has to end."

"Big *if*," says Doreen, raising a cautionary finger. "Because remember, even if the Bomb falls, there'll still be after the Bomb."

After the Bomb?

"Nature's going to win, the world will go on. One thing's

sure—someday there's bound to be total nuclear disarmament, with or without people."

I look at smiling, unflappable Doreen carrying us past the present dangers, beyond the rainbow, right over the edge of the world. Elated, I begin to laugh. Soon we collapse laughing, tears streaming from our eyes. When we recover, I drink to her and to the next story, *After the Bomb*.

THE dry spell lasts another week, then all of a sudden it's trying to rain. The sky blackens; lightning and thunder pierce the sky; winds whip around the bays and break into the house, blowing hats off their hooks. On it goes like a frustrated lover, thrashing this way and that, tensing up, crying out, but try as it may, nothing comes; it can't seem to rain.

After Labor Day, when most of the summer people leave, the southern hurricanes begin. Now the days grow shorter, light and driftwood more precious, solitude more expansive. The nights bring crickets, certain large low-flying squawking birds, the low hiss of the gaslights, and eventually a huge orange harvest moon. The time of moon-shell steaks and sea-urchin roe, the time when wild animals that live hidden amid the summer people begin to make their rare appearances, reclaiming their ground—like the doe, tall as a woman, I see standing on the dunes at the edge of the grasses for two full minutes before she turns and bounds into the woods. Hurricane Harold, after bashing Puerto Rico, sends its stormy messengers shuddering up the coast. Breakers crash against the shore; winds moan; the Coast Guard goes on alert. At last the sky falls and the earth moves as rain pours down in sheets as wide as the world.

And then as suddenly it's Indian summer, and Sarah and Richard Mann, holding hands like young lovers, their two daughters beside them, walk out to the nubble with a package for me. Leaving the children to play in the sand, they climb the stairs and hand me three pounds of venison Richard shot out of season, gift wrapped in the story of the hunt:

A lobsterman spotted a large stag with tremendous antlers ("This big," says Richard, spreading his enormous hands) swimming in toward shore near the ferry landing. He radioed to two more lobstermen out in their boats and together the three moved in on the deer from different sides, corraling it toward land. Finding itself surrounded, the stag panicked and scrambled blindly onto shore, breaking a leg in its charge up the rocks. The lobstermen called in the constable, who reluctantly sentenced the creature, now mortally injured, to be shot, even though hunting season was a month away. Lacking the heart to do the job himself, the constable summoned Richard, who possessed both rifle and license, offering the deer in exchange for the deed. "Done," said Richard, raising the rifle to his shoulder. The stag was so big that, butchered and dressed, it overflowed the freezer. So here, in appreciation of my apple chutneys and seaweed pickles, is a roast for me.

I blanch at the chilling story of a life so carelessly taken, even as I thank my benefactors for their gift. It will be the first red meat I've had on the island since my hamburger days with Jerry, the first venison I've ever cooked. Perfect timing, too: the weather is bound to turn cold again soon, and I'm half expecting Margaret, who has offered to help me close up the cabin.

"It's neck meat," advises Sarah. "With tough cuts like this, I usually just stew the bejesus out of it."

As soon as they leave I open the package. A plump red roast, solid and lean, with a gamy aroma. I pull cookbooks from the shelf and begin my search for inspiration. There's almost nothing on venison, so I settle into the beef sections. Stewing, like pot roasting, means long slow cooking in liquid. Among the various stews and pot roasts are versions for the top of the stove and others for the oven (in case you need to have the oven going anyway). Some require marinating, some do not, and among the marinades some call for wine, some beer, some fruit juices, some vinegar, depending on what you have on hand; likewise with herbs and garnishes. I slowly turn the pages, appreciating anew how most ethnic dishes (including my nubble cuisine) are simply variations on basic food combinations evolved to utilize local and seasonal ingredients. The logic of recipes resembles the logic of life—not: you go to the store and choose what to have, but: how can you utilize what you've been given?

To insure that my meat turns out tender—sometimes a problem with wild game—I select a version of sauerbraten, which entails marinating for at least a week, as I learned to do in Munich that first year I lived abroad shortly after the war when I fell in love with food. I cruise the dunes collecting ingredients for the marinade—fresh juniper berries, half a dozen new bay leaves, a handful of rose hips, angelica, sea rocket, and pods of charlock, which has now gone to seed—and I stir them, along with garlic and onion, into the dregs of a bottle of vinegar diluted by half. Twice a day for a week, at lunch and bedtime, I turn the venison, urging the acidic bath to break down the cell walls and effect an exchange of essences.

Toward the end of the week, as I'm collecting kelp shortly after dawn, I see a red fox tear diagonally up the beach toward the woods. The other fox came at night, but now it's morning, and I take in every detail down to the white hairs on its underbelly. Big, decidedly red, with a long bushy white-fringed tail, pointed nose, large ears—*Margaret*, I think. And the next day, there she is, coming across the beach with her shopping bags.

On the ferry Margaret has heard that the woods are filled with wild mushrooms, now at their peak of autumn abundance. Far from Chernobyl, we decide to try our luck. We read aloud the safety rules in my field guide, then, in boots and fisherman's gloves, set off for the damp woods.

Fungi are everywhere—growing out of the trunks of trees, on stumps, in the underbrush, near puddles, even along the narrow footpath. As we've pledged utter caution—one mistake can be fatal—we pass them by after a look. A silent hour goes by. Then Margaret stoops down before something bright as a marigold under a stand of evergreens.

"This may be a chanterelle," she whispers, as if she's trying not to alarm it. We peer under the delicate indented cap. I open the book. The trumpet shape, the color, the cap's wavy margin, the long descending blunt-edged gills—they seem unmistakable; still . . .

Using her glove, Margaret plucks the fine body from the ground and passes it under her nose.

"What do you think?" I ask.

Smiling, Margaret holds it out to me. "Smell."

Like chanterelles, it has all the fragrance of the earth, with a faint tinge of apricots. And now, by the same magic that reveals to me shellfish, seaweeds, salads, and even the tiny pineapple weed, the invisible becomes visible. Around us, dispersed among the needles, chanterelles begin to appear—some tiny, some substantial, some damaged, but all flaxen or orange, with that pure woodsy essence. We pick all we can find, laying them in our brown paper bags.

"Is that rain?" asks Margaret, holding out a hand. The drops are so fine that they barely patter on the leafy canopy, and although to me all island weather is pure joy, I concede that maybe we'd better head back. We close the bags and retrace our steps. In the small clearing between the woods and the dunes, I spot two giant puffballs—white, huge, smooth as kid gloves. I place them carefully in my bag.

We take off our muddy boots and walk barefoot through the sand and mist. A breeze sends little eddies of sand whirling across the beach and whips the goldenrod into shimmering waves. Back in the cabin we follow the book's instructions, prudently resisting a taste until after we've taken spore prints (of the chanterelles, but not the puffballs, since there's nothing else remotely like puffballs, and "no poisonous species are known"). I lay three chanterelles on clean brown paper to catch the spores that will fall overnight.

The spores are pale yellow, as predicted. We'll eat a puffball omelette for lunch and have chanterelles with our venison.

THE meat is ready to be cooked. And just in time, for the world has turned cold, the alder leaves have curled up and darkened, and the maples on the distant ridge are a blaze of color. With frost predicted, we bring in the last green tomatoes and set them on the windowsill. I sear the roast in the pot on top of the stove until it's brown all over while Margaret slices up onions. These I add to the pot along with the last of the serviceberries, the few precious cranberries I found in a bog, a tomato, and a fresh bouquet garni of nubble herbs, then strain in the fragrant marinade. I set the pot, covered, in the oven, leaving room alongside and below for a bulgur pilaf and an apfelkuchen made of roadside apples.

While the pot simmers, Margaret and I settle down in

front of the fire beneath the antique stag head and talk about meat. How much healthier it seems to eat this stag than the sorry, tortured, hormone-drenched animals raised for slaughter and sold at butcher counters. New scandals about the bacterial contamination of assembly-line meat and poultry surface every month. Even eggs are so loaded with salmonella that you can't eat a raw one anymore, though raw eggs are essential to mayonnaise, ice cream, and Caesar salad; don't even lick the spoon from cookie dough containing egg. No more rare meat or poultry if you want to be safe, no sushi or oyster cocktails, goodbye to sunny-side-up and soft-boiled eggs. But this wild stag must be safe.

And ecologically harmless, observes Margaret, pointing out that our stag—unlike domestic cattle which graze in clear-cut fields of former rain forests or, in the United States, consume in feedlots ten times more grain than people eat directly—has foraged in the woods, like us.

Finally the moment arrives. Margaret sautées the chanterelles while I arrange asters and rose hips for a centerpiece, wishing Charles were with us.

When we take the roast from the oven and open the pot, essence of wildness flows into the room. The meat has turned a lush dark burgundy with henna highlights. Most of the liquid has cooked away. Adding water to the almost blackened concentrate that coats the pot is like pouring in a magic elixir. As I scrape the pot with a wooden spoon to dissolve the precious particles, the liquid and solids mingle into a dark brown velvety gravy, rich with bouquet. We sniff and taste. It needs nothing more, not even a dash of salt.

We cut four slices off the wide end, bathe them in gravy, and, after adding bulgur and greens to the plates, bring them to the table where the sautéed chanterelles await us. Never, before or since, have I eaten such delectable roasted meat, so bold, lean, bursting with flavor. Is it due to the inherent difference between venison and beef, or to the degradation of commercial food which the overwhelming push for profits has stripped of flavor through breeding, processing, and manipulation? For a moment we lament the fate of our common foods—not only beef but eggs, tomatoes, grapes, strawberries, lettuce, and so much else—bred to decadence and now routinely poisoned, nuked, contaminated, irradiated, chemically blitzed, and hormonally zapped. Our grace is a silent moment for the venison that was once so plentiful on this continent and for the passenger pigeon, now extinct, whose mile-long flocks once literally darkened the skies.

Before covering the roast for the night and setting it outside to chill in its iron pot, I estimate how many servings are left, reminding Margaret that a pot roast is always better on the second or third day, after it's had a chance to mature.

"Just like us," says Margaret.

Now the wind is blowing hard, the shrubs and branches are shaking and shedding. The wild roses have gone to seed, turning the bushes red again, with tomato-red hips and leaves the color of burgundy. This is the best time to pick the hips, when the Vitamin C has peaked and the flavor has mellowed, following the first frost—the same frost that destroys most cultivated fruits, so much less hardy. My days here are once again numbered as I frugally plan to use up the last potato, onion, egg. Hoping to return in spring, but not daring to count on it.

Saturday morning we gather rockweed from the beach and spread it over the garden, giving back to the soil what I've taken out. After lunch, while Margaret rests, I hike to the pay phone to make my final round of calls: first the airline, then my parents, children, and lover.

Charles reads me a clipping headlined POISONED MOOSE MEAT: " 'In Maine and Ontario, hunters are being advised not to eat moose livers because they contain high levels of cadmium, while in the Northeast, waterfowlers are advised not to eat geese and ducks because of high levels of PCBs.' "

"So!" I cry. "Even if the mushrooms are safe this time, they got us on the meat." Though I missed Charles at our banquet, now I'm glad he was spared.

"But," he says, sliding to the rescue with a compassionate distinction, "this is about *moose*, not deer"—stretching compassion to a fault. (*Idiot compassion*, Gurdjieff calls it because it hides the truth.) He reads on: " 'The cleanest air and water—and by extension the least contaminated game—can be found in the Great Plains and the mountainous West. As one heads downstream from the Divide, through agricultural lands and industrial areas, the aggregation of pollutants increases until one reaches the Great Lakes and the coasts. Because they serve as sinks for the rest of the continent, these aquatic environments and their inhabitants tend to be the most polluted.' "

"Aquatic environments and their inhabitants—I suppose that means me."

"I suppose it does—though actually, if you think about it," he says, trying to cheer me, "islands are mountaintops."

However endearing Charles's wild generous attempts at consolation, they are utterly useless as each day it grows clearer that everyone is implicated, no matter what your altitude or elevation. It no longer takes a mystic to know that, at bottom, all mountains are connected. Not even an island is an island.

"WHAT's that, do you suppose?" asks Margaret, pointing to the ocean as I hammer nails into the shutters.

"What?"

"Out there. That foam on the waves."

Far out, a murky yellow foam, like the scum on pea soup, is moving slowly toward shore. Until this year I might have speculated that it's one of the wonders of nature—perhaps something creative, like fish spawn. Now I don't know what to think. The foam, like a vast pool of floating vomit, draws closer, spreads. As it approaches the Shmoos I remember an oil slick of a dozen years ago that coated some of the rocks with a black film that kept us from walking out to Dedgers barefoot. If you got some of it on your clothes it never came off. Stevie got some in his hair, and when it wouldn't wash out I had to cut it off.

The scum breaks into ten thousand bubbles of foam as it hits the rocks, then disappears. Relieved, I resume boarding up—until Margaret points again toward the horizon where another slick of yellow spume—this one twice as large as the last—is riding the swells toward shore.

TWELVE

. . . O you who love clear edges
more than anything   watch the edges that blur
—ADRIENNE RICH

AN ecotone is an environmental edge where two systems meet. It is here at the edge that species stretch their limits and extend their range, creating entirely new forms. Once I understood how the island and the world had met, I knew the time had come to stretch my own limits and extend my range. Especially on the eve of a new book.

Having grown used to working on a computer, I debated buying one of the new battery-operated laptops for the nubble. I hoped eventually to run it by solar energy; but meanwhile I asked Mat Burns if he might build me a drawer beneath his house where for a fee I could plug it into his power supply and recharge it while I slept. I knew I'd be plugging back into clock time with all its attendant anxiety (can I finish the scene and save my files before the battery goes dead?), but doesn't wholeness require that one be in oneself and the world at once? In the end, this was where my long journey through solitude had brought me: back to the world, ready to test my flexibility.

But was bringing in a laptop flexibility or hypocrisy?

Extending my range or (that Fifties bugaboo) selling out? I spent a long time puzzling over the impact and meaning of a laptop on the island, as if low-tech living were my religion, suddenly provoking a crisis of faith. Which made no sense: after all, in the city I work on a computer, and even on the nubble I've always appreciated my propane for cooking and light. If on chilly nights I sometimes wear a nightcap to bed and pee in a chamber pot, it's because these are simple, efficient solutions to practical problems. But whenever the weather turns so cold that I must shiver before a fire from dawn till dawn, I'm glad to leave my drafty cabin for the overheated blare of the brashest city in the East, then shuttle back and forth between my two great loves like a man who will give up neither wife nor mistress. Over my city desk I've always kept a photo of the nubble, showing the children as toddlers playing on an empty beach at low tide, while over my nubble desk hangs an expanding row of postcards of New York City: the skyline, the Brooklyn Bridge, Mulberry Street at festival time, Fifth Avenue seen from Central Park, and my favorite, a crowded graffiti-filled subway car—the kind where, long before I came alone to the nubble, my first mystical vision occurred. Above the postcards hangs a six-foot-long World History Chart stretching from 4000 B.C. to the present, bringing human history at a glance (via fifteen parallel time lines, each representing a civilization) to this timeless spot. The wall itself resembles an ecotone where past and future, city and seaside meet. If this shuttling back and forth condemns me to the despised category of Summer Person, well, worse epithets have been flung at me. Why not add *sellout* to the list and get a laptop?

More troubling was the question of what to write. I was always urging my students: write about what matters to you most, about what you know best. Could I ask less of myself? The subject that had stretched my imagination and stirred my passions, changing the way I think of New Age, middle age, and old age, transforming me from spooked to game, altering the very way I see, was precisely the life I practice here. But how could I possibly write about it? First, to do so might jinx it by letting ego, which had quietly slipped away as I lived unobserved, sneak back in and jeopardize my joy—like one of those "happenings" in which a work of art self-destructs. Second, what approach could I use? What tense?—here where there's only the present. What genre? A solitary life with only one character hardly seemed the stuff of fiction. A memoir, then? A meditation on solitude, first-person solipsist? But I was usually reluctant even to discuss my solitary low-tech existence, afraid to sound righteous or proud, which never goes unpunished, or worse, privileged, utopian, irrelevant. ("No *electricity*? No *telephone*?" Certain friends had been indignant at my refusal in the city of a mere answering machine—nothing compared to having no phone at all.) Why submit my secret life to judgment by putting it on display? The rest of my doubts came crowding in, picketing my will, censoring my hopes, laying a trap of writer's block.

In my struggle I pulled out my dog-eared copy of Helen and Scott Nearing's classic *Living the Good Life*, which in the final chapter (pointedly called "A Balance Sheet") proposes no fewer than six separate justifications for their moving to an "idyllic spot" in Vermont instead of remaining in the city to "shar[e] the misery and anguish of our fellow human beings"—justifications ranging from weighty ("as a desirable, limited alternative to one segment of the existing social order") to touching ("as a milieu in which heretofore active people can spend their riper years") to quaint ("as a refuge for political deviants") to inspiring ("as an example of sane living in an insane world") to personal ("as a means of contacting nature")—all serious, all applicable, all as peculiarly American as the need to justify, itself.

The next time Charles came out to visit I asked him offhandedly, "Do you ever wonder how to justify your life?"

At that moment he was splitting driftwood logs and stacking them in the shed, trying to make himself indispensable. He rested the ax deep in a log, crossed his arms, and looked at me suspiciously. "You mean, what I do? How do I justify what I do? Is that what you mean?"

From the edge in his voice I knew he thought *I* was judging *him*. "No, no, no," I rushed to assure him. "I don't mean you. I mean, must one justify one's life or does it justify itself—existence for its own sake?"

A curtain of puzzlement crossed his face as he slowly shook his head. "That something you think about often?"

I nodded. "Don't you?"

"Never. Not in a million years would it occur to me to ask a question like that."

Still, I brooded, and continued to brood after he left until I was visited by the encouraging voices of a few wise friends:

"Privilege?" snaps Hope the poet-activist, raven eyes flashing, in response to my scruple about my privileged existence. "You know what to do with privilege? Use it for our side. It's a blessing to be used. The only bad thing about privilege is to waste it! Besides," she points out, "you're judged not by a part of your life but by all of it." (Does this mean, I wonder, that I can coast through half the year on the virtues I practice in the other half? If so, which is the virtuous half?)

And here's Thoreau, that master solitaire, who knows that every life is relevant. "Why should we exaggerate any one kind at the expense of others?" he asks, adding, "I desire that there be as many different persons in the world as possible."

Even Elizabeth Cady Stanton, feminist fighter extraordinaire, insists that "to develop our real selves, we need time alone for thought and meditation. To be always giving out and never pumping in, the well runs dry."

But it's Margaret's voice that convinces me. "Bliss is always a gift, wherever you find it. How you get it is your own business."

And indeed, much of the joy I always feel on the island lies precisely in being free of the nagging suspicion I used to have that no matter what I was doing I might better be doing something else: if playing with my kids I should be working, if working I was neglecting my friends, if out with my friends I belonged home with my kids. How often I accused myself of reading when I ought to be writing, of writing when I ought to be reading, of staying indoors when I ought to be out in the streets . . . filling my ears with *oughts*, but never knowing which ear the devil was whispering in.

"Don't you see?" I hear Margaret say. "You're always in equal danger of falling off either side of the tightrope. So you'd better just trust yourself and keep moving along on your own course, without letting anyone dissuade you." I remember the time, when I was pregnant with Amy, I left Stevie with my parents while Jerry and I went off for a week of fishing. I didn't want to leave him, he was only a year old, but Jerry was quite insistent; and since it was our first separation, Stevie's and mine, and I didn't know how I'd feel, I went along with Jerry. The first day I was uncomfortable; by the second day I was wretched. What was I doing out there in a boat catching sunfish in the middle of a lake without my child? I told Jerry I was going back. He was miffed, but he couldn't stop me. After that, I never went fishing again. "If you want to write this book," says Margaret, "just write it."

"But on a laptop?" I counter slyly, devil's advocate. "What will people think if I use a computer to praise the virtues of simplicity?"

Before the question's even half formed Margaret's laughter fills my head as she delivers the final, indisputable argument: "Pardon me, I thought the main reason you're here is so you can do what you want without having to worry about what people think."

Yes, for me that was the blessing of the nubble and of passing fifty into solitude: knowing that you are your own final judge. Despite the losses, guilts, and fears you can never completely shake, you're on your own, along with everyone else.

Writing, that ultimate effort to recycle, has always made my world more real for me, not less so. Secret love is fragile, but true love should be able to withstand exposure. If my love affair with solitude that had miraculously returned me to the arms of the world couldn't survive the telling, it was time to find out.

BAREFOOT, knees drawn up, I'm sitting on a rock at Dedgers on a chill, breezy day following a thought as it loops and soars with the gulls tilting on the currents, economizing with the wind. It's ten years since I first came here alone to learn the shape of possibility. I'm sixty, my face is lined, my left knee is acting up; yet my feelings of oneness with the dense pullulating life around me keep deepening. Each test I've encountered on my decade-long journey—my comrades' disappointments, my children's doubts, love's sweet allure, the gathering threats to life—only strengthens me. The air is sweet, the sea is blue. Off beyond the outhouse, near the insulated studio that Richard Mann has built for me so I can stretch the season and have a place to work when Margaret or Charles or the children visit, swallows dart after bugs. A black-faced gull comes swooping toward me, and I know if I'm patient enough the great blue heron will come too. Breakers crashing at my feet, connecting me with every ocean shore on earth, swell into waves of love.

As I calmly wait for the heron, I recall the time the hacker finally arrived on the nubble (like the gun Chekhov famously said must go off by the end of Act III if it hangs on the wall in Act I), smashing a window into jagged fragments and forcing the door of the new studio, where I'd locked up my laptop and manuscripts during Jerry's annual visit. I was off the island teaching a workshop when he came. When I returned to face the terrifying black hole where the window belonged and slivers of glass strewn everywhere, I learned from Mat Burns's son that the vandal was none other than Jerry himself, who had indulged his rage at being locked out of the studio by smashing the window with his baseball bat. So the weapon he intended as protection against intruders was in the end wielded by the hacker himself.

Now, munching a strand of arame, I ponder again the paradox James Baldwin set me my first summer here alone, a paradox that has become my credo: "To hold in the mind forever two ideas which seemed to be in opposition. The first . . . acceptance totally without rancor, of life as it is, and men as they are[;] . . . the second . . . that one must never, in one's own life, accept . . . injustices as commonplace but must fight them with all one's strength." The thought continues to stretch and lengthen, snaking across the nubble and wreathing around the world until a luminous clarity comes over me. I now know that Baldwin's two are really one, acceptance and struggle two sides of a single necessity. For me the first idea is the cause of the second, my acceptance and love of this life making passivity impossible. The more I love it the more I care about its fate, our fate, want to protect the suffering seas, the weeds, the air, the spawn, and each neglected old woman. But equally for me, the second is the cause of the first. For, from my first embrace of our soul-stirring movement at the dawn of my adulthood, fighting injustice was my main path into the world, my connection with each living soul, the way I came to write, to know myself, and to love the world.

I never sprayed the apple tree. If once I began, where would it end? Instead, I learned to live with the larvae of the brown-tail moth, killing only those few I found inside the cabin. They disappeared for a few seasons after that first summer; then I moved to Hawaii (where the mountains were full of wild ginger, passion fruit, figs, avocados, mangoes, and guavas that rolled at my feet); then the larvae returned; then I did. Through it all, the tree survived, leafing out every spring, though it did stop fruiting ("Like us," Margaret would probably say)—at least for a while.

This is not unjust. There are always enough roadside apples for my pies, and, between the elderberries whose white umbels spread around the front deck, the serviceberry bushes growing beyond the outhouse, and the new blackberry canes that sprang up on the plot of my onetime garden, I never lack for fruit. And every year, whenever I have the yen, I study my books and discover some new delicious vegetable that has been there all along, growing practically up to my door—like the succulent green goosetongues, or seaside plantains, those long slender stemless spikes tasting like a cross between snap beans and artichokes that grow seemingly without soil at every crack or fissure in the rocks where nothing else survives.

Adapting, I slather on sunblock here at Dedgers—and also on city streets in winter where I sometimes hand out leaflets with my aging sisters whose faith has been rewarded by a groundswell of young activists (also now wearing tennis shoes, even with their tailored suits) calling themselves Ecofeminists and the Third Wave. I've cut down on my mussels to twice a month, at the full moon and the new moon, and force them to flush the pollutants from their stomachs by the age-old method of adding a handful of cornmeal to their water an hour before cooking.

When I first came here I thought it would be a tragedy to be stopped dead in the middle of writing a book—all that wasted work, the meanings you'd been struggling for left forever unsaid. But now I think it may be best to end, as it is to begin, in medias res, somewhere in the middle—which is to say, passionately engaged with what matters most to you. Or as Margaret, who is fast approaching seventy-five, is fond of observing, *Since this story is endless, I might as well end it here.*

As of this writing, the Bomb hasn't fallen, and the outhouse, which has served for three decades without a cleaning, shows no sign of filling up. Perhaps the tides will heal the hole in the world.